The Girl in the
Gold Bikini

My Turbulent Journey
Through Food and Family

Dana Goldstein

Cover Design by JWedholm Design

Editing by Zoey Duncan zoeyduncan.com

Quote on Page 23: "Self-worth shouldn't be measured in pounds" is courtesy of Marci Warhaft. Visit www.fitvsfiction.com

ISBN-13: 978-1-7751438-0-2

DEDICATION

For Jeff, Mason and Westin.
There is only you.
You are my lighthouse, my fire, my grounding wire.
Don't stop hugging me. Like, ever.

Table of Contents

Introduction

I first started writing this book as an experiment. I've been hefty all my life and writing has always been cathartic for me. Since Grade 9, I've wanted to write a book. This was before computers and word-processing software existed, so all my writing happened in shitty notebooks that were either poorly stapled and fell apart, or were coil bound and dug into the fleshy side of my left hand as I wrote. When I started this book in January 2017, I was writing with the hope that by pounding my angst into the keyboard I would miraculously start losing weight. My vision was that as I released my pain, and vilified those who had a hand in perpetuating it, I would easily and without effort release 10, 20, 50 and then 100 pounds of flab that my body was holding on to like a shield.

Yeah, that didn't happen at all.

In fact, I gained 13 pounds in the first two months of writing. With every new chapter, I felt good about the writing, but still shitty about my waistline. I kept writing and bought bigger pants.

Eventually, some weight did start to fall off. By the time my third draft was done, I had lost 10 of the 13 pounds I'd gained. In my mind, I began building a course, one that my skinny self would teach, and I gave it a Fox News-worthy title: Write Off the Weight (or "How to channel your anger into a book that will piss off your family and make you skinny again").

I'm not there yet, and I am still fighting to lose weight. What this book has become is an examination into why I eat what I do, how it makes me feel and why I need food as a crutch. Stick with me through my journey. You'll undoubtedly recognize some of yourself in these anecdotes, but if you don't, at the very least, I hope you'll enjoy the stories. And maybe my insight will trigger some revelations in your own eating habits and spur you into action.

— With love (and chocolate), Dana

MILK & COOKIES

1 THE AWAKENING

My horrible relationship with food — and with myself — began when I was a latchkey kid, sitting at home after school with nothing but homework and the echoes of the hurtful words of others bouncing around in my brain between math problems. My single, working mother did the best she could with the tools she had: an overbearing personality, a sense of entitlement and an endless supply of bitterness. Her best left me craving compassion, empathy, encouragement and salty foods.

You know you have a problem when you wake up at 7 a.m. on a Sunday and your first thought is "potato chips." Before I even put coffee to my lips, I'm on my phone, looking up which grocery store opens earliest so I can go satiate my craving. I learn I've got two hours until the store opens and I'm devastated that I have to wait that long. In my head, a battle is brewing between the sensible side that says, *You know this is crazy, right?* and the willful side that screams, *CHIPS, CHIPS, CHIPS … and dip.* On the bright side, I've got two hours to rationalize. That doesn't mean I talk myself out of getting dressed, and sneaking away to the grocery store while my kids are still sleeping and scoring some chips and dip. Rationalizing is figuring out what else I can buy so I don't look like an addict who needs potato chips at 9 a.m. on Sunday morning.

I'm standing in my kitchen, searching the fully stocked pantry, looking for the missing items that can justify the trip. I only need one or two reasonable items so the cashier will not judge the early-morning purchase of a family-size bag of all-dressed and a small container of French onion dip. Please Lord, let the pantry be devoid of a can of chicken noodle soup. There is nothing to put on the grocery list since my husband took care of the groceries on Friday. I decide to sit on the couch with my coffee and a book, hoping to distract myself from the craving. Sometimes, I'll last almost 10 minutes before I give in to the voices that don't quiet down. While I'm reading, I'm also mentally categorizing what is in the fridge:

Milk.

Orange juice.

Yogurt.

Salad fixings.

Cottage cheese.

Fruit.

Cheese.

Leftovers.

Turkey sticks.

Wait — is there lunch meat? I get up to look in the fridge drawer where we store our lunch meats. I am fully relieved to see we neglected to replenish the deli meats that will make up the lunches for the week. Now I'll look like a frazzled mom who realized she didn't have what she needed to make lunches and decided to get some snacks for a football game later that afternoon. Naturally, that is exactly what the cashier will think.

Somewhere along the way, maybe because of too much reality TV, I've come to believe that skinny people are as obsessed with my weight as I am. But that's just a bullshit story in my head.

I've worked in the entertainment industry, and I know these "reality" shows are staged. It may seem like people are making random, nasty comments — and they are — but what you don't see is the TV lackey planted in the situation who makes the initial remark, goading others to say something too. And people usually jump on board to say hurtful, mean things. I don't think human beings are naturally malicious, I think we all want a sense of belonging, even if that happens at the expense of others.

The other thing I know is that the obese don't encounter 15 nasty people in a day. Don't get me wrong, I have had my share of hateful comments tossed my way, but for the most part, people are just too involved in their own drama to really give a shit about the fat girl in the lobby. I am certain that people view me differently because of the girth of my hips. I know I have lost work to a less-talented but skinny person. I know my work ethic has been questioned as a reflection of my lack of self-control. But it doesn't all happen in the same day.

What does happen on a daily basis is I conjure horrible imagined conversations in my head.

The lady at the convenience store is probably about to say: *You know, you'd be better off just buying some water and some gum.*

The patient I'm recording at an appointment: *I guess I should be grateful I haven't ballooned like her.*

The girl at the green juice kiosk: *Really? I'm not sure you are representative of the kind of customer we want.*

The people in the elevator: *Fuck, are we going over capacity?*

This dialogue inside my head happens everywhere I go. I know eyes are on me. I watch people, their eyes skimming over my body, a brief change in the eyes, eyebrows frowning for a split second, mouth dropping a bit in shock, shoulders sagging with either relief or concern. Discrimination is not always verbal. I'm not imagining these things, I am tuned into the subtleties of body language. I've had a lifetime of practice.

For as long as I can remember, a large bag of chips has been my go-to when I am bored, lonely or trying to not deal with what is really hurting me. I don't mindlessly eat a bag; I savour each one, nibbling away at the ridges as if I can chew my way through my feelings. When the bag is done, whatever triggered the binge is forgotten, but I am left dealing with the guilt of the fat and calories I just consumed. Again.

I went to a private Jewish school — heavily subsidized — where I learned not only proper grammar, but that I was poor, that our apartment was less than glorious and that being the child of divorce was stigmatized. My husband always says I have a chip on my shoulder when it comes to wealthy, skinny Jews, and he's right. I can't shake what years of not having the right clothes, of being judged not only by my peers, but by the teachers who were supposed to protect me while expanding my mind, did to me. Day after day, I took the long bus ride to the other end of the city and got home to an empty apartment. I was bored and lonely, but that's only part of the reason I began to eat. Sweets and salty snacks made me feel good. I was happy while I was eating, watching an after-school special, completely unaware of the volume of food I was consuming.

If I ate too much, which I usually did, my mother would berate me. I used to think she was angry with me for just snacking so much; I now realize she was pissed because I ate *her* snacks. As I got older, I rationalized that I might as well finish the whole bag of chips or devour the final row of cookies. The consequences would be the same regardless of how much I consumed: I would feel guilty and sick and I would get yelled at and be made to feel worse. I would like to say that if my mother had just taken a few minutes to really talk *with* me, to discover what my day was like, to take an interest in what I was feeling, then maybe things would have turned out different. She faced so many challenges: parents who were not affectionate, a marriage she hoped would help her escape from her own pain, a husband who gambled and became unavailable after I arrived. All she had, really, was me, and I was not an easy kid. I was smarter than her, she didn't understand my humour and I was the spitting image of my father — a daily reminder of her failings.

If I had sought professional help when I was in my 20s, I'd probably be a size eight or 10 right now. I'd probably have healthy eating habits. I'd most definitely have had a different trajectory to my life. I've finally learned to trust my husband of 13 years with my inner thoughts and feelings, shaking off a lifetime of having my pain thrown back in my face by those I loved. But I've had a pretty spectacular adult life so far — spectacularly weird and fascinating and awe-inspiring — regardless of the width of my hips.

2 THE FIRST DIET

I was put on my first diet at 10 years old. My mother was always obsessed with her weight — and mine. She was fond of reminding me that I was a skinny kid until I was four or five and then I "just started gaining weight." To her, this was how you motivated someone. Since I was incapable of losing the weight on my own, and misery loves company, my mother took me to Weight Watchers.

The meetings were held in a community centre not far from our north Toronto apartment. It was the winter of 1980 — dull and cold — and the building blended right into the blah. We entered through a side door, like fat people were not invited to use the front door, but were required to surreptitiously enter where we wouldn't be seen. To top it off, the meeting was held in the basement. I was the *only* child in the room, and I felt sorely out of place, like I was in a space where children were not welcome. While my mom registered, I tried to make myself invisible by not looking at anyone, being interested in the floor and my shoes. I noticed the grey concrete walls, the beige and metal utility chairs, the other women in the room. I did not make eye contact with anyone. Even at 10, I felt embarrassed about being there. When my mother finished with registration, I silently moved toward the chairs.

"Not yet, young lady," said an unfamiliar voice, one of the meeting staff. "You need to come over here and get yourself weighed."

What? Here? In front of everybody?

Confused, I did not move. My mother gave me a shove from

behind, guiding me toward a medical scale against a wall near the registration table. "Take your shoes off," my mother instructed.

I felt my face burning when I stepped on that scale. I had no idea how much I weighed, nor did I have any idea of what I was supposed to weigh. All I knew, from the clucking tongues and shaking heads, is that I weighed more than these adults thought was acceptable. I was mortified that all these strangers saw my number and became part of my shame.

I zoned out for the rest of the hour. I had no idea what my mother weighed, what the people in the room were talking about or what the leader was sharing. I sat, trying so hard not to cry, wishing for the horrible experience to be over. I was lost in my thoughts, wondering what was wrong with me, why I couldn't be skinny like the other girls in school. I felt like I was being punished for the extra bulge around my middle. *Maybe it's not baby fat, like my babysitter once said. Maybe my mother will love me more when I am thin. Maybe my dad will come back.* My little, magical, 10-year-old world shifted into the adult space I wasn't supposed to have to worry about yet. Giving a 10-year-old the impression that her body is somehow wrong sets her up for a lifetime of body-weight issues, from bingeing and purging, to extreme weight loss. No weighing and measuring her food, or examining the contents of her lunchbox and wanting to cry over the anticipated hunger that she knows will make for a very long day at school. Nobody ever wanted to trade cookies for a box of raisins or an apple.

I walked out of that meeting overcome with shame. Back in the car, my mother said, "I hope you like apples and celery, because that's all you're going to be able to eat." She was snarling. As she put the car in drive and headed home, I turned my head to look out the window. I started to cry. Silently, so my mother didn't know and had no reason to ridicule me further.

3 DANCING

It's just a stupid machine. A small thing really. It's nothing more than a series of dials and numbers, but it has immense power.

The scale. I hate this fucking machine. It plays head games with everyone. There is no discrimination between sex, race, age. The scale can reduce the strongest person to a puddle of tears. A pool of anxiety.

It's amazing to me just how much influence the scale has on my day. Of all my bad relationships, the one I have with the scale is the one I haven't let go of, and it's the most toxic. Even when I was at my skinniest, collarbones sticking out and my neck looking like it couldn't support my head, I looked to the scale for support. No matter what I did, the scale made me feel like crap. If I had a good week, eating healthy, feeling strong, my underwear digging into me a little less, the scale would take that away when it showed either no loss or an increase. If I had a tough week, emotionally crippling, filled with bad food choices, the scale would exacerbate my anguish by confirming that, *Yes, you will never lose the weight*. It's an ugly, hateful machine.

I have a really smart friend who says, "Self-worth shouldn't be measured in pounds," but the scale has been my value meter since the age of 10. I know people who join weight-loss programs and refuse to get weighed facing the scale. They don't want to see the numbers, as if that will change reality. There is such denial around the scale. I've played horrible games with the scale: weighing myself before and after going to the bathroom to see if I can manipulate the number to move one notch lower; weighing myself with my clothes on and conveniently "forgetting" that the following week when I step on the scale in bra and panties; moving the scale to other parts of the bathroom to test where I can get the lowest number.

Whenever I step on the scale, one of two things happen: I either let out a small puff of breath, one that rounds my shoulders down in defeat, or I smile for a brief moment, feeling like I have dodged a bullet. My relationship with the scale is like a friendship with someone who is completely unpredictable. I tiptoe around, hoping I don't accidentally trigger a reaction. The negative sticks with me all day; I take the positive with a grain of salt, knowing that it's only a matter of time until I am the target of vitriol once again.

It's ridiculous how a small device that shares space with a toilet can cause such anxiety, defining how I feel about myself. The scale, for me, is a symbol of my relationship with my mother: manipulative, nasty and joy-sucking.

Until I was old enough to make my own choices, my mother enrolled me in every kind of activity she could find that would inspire physical activity. I took dance classes: ballet, jazz and tap. I had weekly swimming lessons, earning every badge right up until the lifeguarding level. I was in gymnastics and running club for a while, both laughable activities for a chubby kid. Our girth is not built for taking on balance beams, track curves or hurdles. I wanted to take creative classes like drama and pottery, but those were not mother-endorsed, weight-loss-achieving programs. My mother sabotaged my artistic outlets in a variety of ways: the class was on a day I already had something else, the class was too expensive, the class was full. I once auditioned for a beginner drama class. After the audition, I heard the instructor tell my mother that I was too advanced for the beginner class, but not quite ready for the next level. She enrolled me in neither.

Twice per week, I took the bus after school to a Jewish community centre in the northern part of the city. All my extracurricular activities happened in that centre. It was there that I discovered the cafeteria (the freshly baked cookies), the freedom of unaccountability (no one cared if you showed up or not), and the trickiness of deceit (my mother would never know if I had skipped gymnastics and watched an art class instead).

The Jewish community centre's dance classes were held in an enormous studio on the second floor. The room was a typical dance space: highly polished oak floors, a wall of mirrors, ballet barres attached to the mirrors. It is here that I felt truly free, learning that my body could move in ways I never imagined. I was in a world where I could be anonymous, since this community centre was at the north end of Toronto, far removed from my school. There would be no jaunts, jeers or judging looks here. I did not know any of the other eight-year-olds in my classes but we all moved to the music as a cohesive unit. If I missed a beat, the rest of the group kept working through the movements. It was up to me to join in when I corrected myself. Jazz dancing was my favourite — I loved the soft leather of the dance shoes and the feeling of not wearing anything at all on my feet. I struggled with ballet, never quite feeling the grace and poise required for the art. I took jazz for a year, ballet for the next year. But tap dancing put me at the top of my dancing game. I found satisfaction in the noise of the taps, and I felt important when I walked in my tap shoes. It was the only dance I practiced at home, after I begged my mother to buy me a tap board. Somehow, she found the money for a two-foot by three-foot piece of ply board. I regularly dragged that board into our living room so I could practice my heel, toe, ball, flat. The rhythm and defined steps of dance gave me a sense of accomplishment.

As my group practiced week after week, we got better, finding our synchronicity, remembering the steps and working as a unit. When I danced, I could feel the music moving through my body. It was a very different feeling from the tension and anxiety I felt in my day-to-day life. Within months, dancing became my best friend.

For years, I practiced, perfected and pirouetted. I knew I'd never be a professional dancer, and when I turned 12, my dance career came to a big finish with the final recital. Our jazz class drew the long straw: not every dance class was invited to participate in the recital, and I was lucky to be enrolled in one that was. When the excitement died down in class, I felt the nerves settle on me like dust falling from the ceiling fans. *What if I screw up? What if I go left when everyone else goes right? I'll have to practice hard and often so I don't let my dance mates down.* It never once occurred to me to be anxious about the audience watching me on stage. I would be performing with the seven other dancers in my jazz class. For the remainder of the academic year, we practiced our movements and our choreography, working hard until we moved with unity. Our instructor was kind and patient, but relentless in repetition. "Again" was her favourite word.

On the night of the recital, I was filled with anxiety. I'd never before appeared on a stage in a real theatre, let alone while wearing makeup and a bedazzled, sequined leotard. Backstage, dancers of all types and from all age groups were practicing, stretching, giggling. The older teenage girls had the confidence that comes with years of practice, coupled with the insecurity of the changes in their bodies.

I was scared I would misstep, throw our whole line off and be laughed at, but when I stepped on stage, I realized the lights made it impossible for me to see anyone at all. As the first few notes played, my brain switched from terrified kid to focused dancer. I counted my steps and beats in my head and performed with pleasure. I wasn't throwing all my passion into the moves, I was methodically delivering. Staying focused on what I was supposed to be doing pulled me away from thinking about the audience. This was not free-form dancing, this was performance. I loved every minute of the structure and attention.

At the end of the evening, as all the dancers emerged from their dressing rooms, stripped of all the makeup and costumes and looking like ordinary teens, I smiled when parents came to embrace their daughters, handing them bouquets of roses. There was praise and hugs all around. I waited for my mother to come greet me, hoping that she had hidden roses in our tiny hatchback and had deftly sneaked them into the theatre. I waited for more than 15 minutes, and when families started to leave, I followed them back into the theatre. I saw my mother standing near the stairs at stage left. No roses. No hugs. No beaming smile. I walked over, smiling with pride, nonetheless.

"So," I started, "what did you think?"

She looked at me, giving me a once-over from head to toe.

"I think it took a lot of guts for you to get on stage in that leotard."

4 MIAMI BEACH

I once had a gold bikini.

I was seven years old and in Miami Beach, Florida, with my mother, grandparents and great-grandparents like a Jewish cliché. We were staying at the National Hotel on Collins Avenue, the same place my maternal grandparents and great-grandparents stayed every winter. In the '70s and '80s, these hotels were far removed from the posh properties that now populate Miami Beach. The hotels were no more than 12 storeys high, their art-deco exteriors and stucco reminding me of the old days I knew nothing about. I'm not sure if the hotels felt ancient because of the structures or the occupants. Every hotel on Collins was on the beach (before Ocean Drive was built and pushed some of the hotels off the beach), and the white sand went on for miles. At the hotel, there was shuffleboard, a swimming pool and lots of old people with flowery bathing caps. I have extremely fond memories of Miami Beach.

The front of the hotel facing Collins Avenue had an enormous, covered veranda where a good portion of the tenants collected in the evening, sitting on chrome and plastic chairs, to share stories and watch the pedestrians go by. The floor of highly polished white quartz looked so beautiful in the evening lights — sparkling and cool — a stark contrast to the heat that rose off the stone during the day. That veranda was always bustling every night. As a distracted kid, I didn't have the patience to sit and listen to the stories the seniors told. I wish I had listened more closely. I am sure there were Holocaust survivors, war veterans and immigrants from old Europe. Now, in my 40s, I know the lessons they could have taught me through their stories would have been fascinating.

I spent winter vacation in Miami Beach for years, from the ages of six to 13. One year, as I sat in the pool area with the plastic strips of the chaise lounge sticking to my legs, I had a short conversation with a gentleman in the chair next to me about whether we preferred the beach (him) or the pool (me). I later found out, through the whisperings of the folks on the veranda, that the man was actor Christopher Plummer. That's what Miami Beach was like back then. The moderately famous celebrities could stay where they wanted, walk among the normal people and not be harassed by paparazzi. Everything about Miami Beach was laid back.

The suite we shared with my grandparents had a full kitchen. My great-grandmother's staple food was baked apples. They had a sweet, slightly acidic smell that permeated the whole apartment. There were always baked apples in the fridge or the oven. Today, a fresh apple pie, or a warm glass of apple cider brings the memories of my great-grandmother flooding back to me. I smell love and acceptance and a matriarch you don't mess with in those apples. I smell family. I miss that wonderful lady.

For eight years, I looked forward to going to Miami Beach. I walked Washington Avenue and Lincoln Road with my grandmother, stopping to look in the electronics superstore windows, looking for deals in Woolworths (and leaving with exotic — to me — chocolate bars we couldn't find in Canada), trying on some new clothes in Lerner's, stopping for drugstore supplies in Fedco. There weren't a lot of kids at the National Hotel. South Miami Beach wasn't attractive to young families back then. Many families stayed further north in Hollywood, closer to Fort Lauderdale and the malls. I felt safe and unjudged by the seniors, who thought nothing of a chubby little girl jumping into the pool in her gold bikini. I had that bikini for two years, and I know it was too small that second year. I didn't care though. I felt like a moderately famous celebrity, blissfully unaware of my protruding belly.

Before we knew the sun was trying to kill us, I walked miles on the beach in that bikini, picking shells and poking the blue-bubbled man o' war, the dome of the National Hotel always clearly visible no matter how far I ventured out. I felt so free during those vacations — free to just be a kid and enjoy being.

5 FIRST GRADE

Finding an appropriate school for a precocious, inquisitive child is a challenge for any parent, but it's extremely complicated for a single mother with a limited income. I am grateful for my mother's tenacious attitude when it came to my education. Bialik Hebrew Day School was an intense, academically focused school that had students from kindergarten to Grade 9. When my mother went to enrol me early in Grade 1, the principal wanted to hold me back because of my age. He did not care that I had skipped junior kindergarten nor was he interested in testing my abilities and knowledge. But my mother was relentless. She spoke to the school board, the vice principal and anyone who was in a position of influence. After putting up her fight, she won, and I was admitted into Grade 1.

My Grade 1 teacher, Miss Day, was brand new to teaching. When I watched her, I could see her newness in her nervousness. She was really easily confused and lost control of the classroom on a regular basis. She had no idea what to do with her unruly students; she had even less of a clue when it came to the advanced ones.

Her big pet peeve was chewing gum. If she caught any of us chewing gum in class, Miss Day would make us stand in a corner of the classroom with the gum stuck to the tip of our nose. I was caught once, chomping away on Dubble Bubble. I wasn't embarrassed by having to stand at the back of the class with pink gum on my nose; it made us all giggle. I only struggled with the sticky feeling I had on my nose for the rest of the day. The great humiliations for a six-year-old, I would discover, were reserved for the playground.

I was restless and bored early in Grade 1. I fidgeted, wrapping my arms and upper body over the top of my desk, kicking my legs up behind me like a swimmer. I chatted with my classmates while lessons were being taught. I was disruptive and distracted, but every time Miss Day called me out and asked me a question, I had the answer. She thought I wasn't listening, but I was absorbing every detail. My problem was that I needed more than she could offer. At report card time, my grades were exemplary. I hit every milestone. I achieved nearly perfect scores on most tests. Only my reading comprehension grades were oddly low.

"There's something wrong with this reading grade," my mother told Miss Day on parent-teacher night.

"No, there isn't. Dana just won't read what she is assigned," Miss Day said. "She looks at the booklet, opens a few pages, then closes it. She stares out the window and then becomes disruptive. I think maybe she needs extra help with reading."

Confused, my mother asked to see what I was reading. Miss Day showed her the booklets: short sentences, large-type words and pictures spread over 20 pages. Pretty much what you'd expect for the beginning of the first grade.

"*This* is what you're giving her?" My mother laughed. "It's no wonder she's wrapping herself around her desk. This is way beneath her reading level. Did it never occur to you to ask Dana to read to you or did you just assume she was illiterate?"

Miss Day blushed and then her humiliation turned into belligerence. "There are very clear indications that Dana cannot read. She needs more help than we can give her here."

My mother, a teacher herself, fired back.

"Can she do math?"

"Yes."

"Does she do well on those tests?"

"Yes."

"Does she pay attention in science?"

"Yes."

"I see her test marks for science are high."

"Yes."

"Does she participate in class?"

"Well, see, that's the thing. Dana looks like she's not even listening, but when I ask her a question about what we are discussing in class, she *always* has the correct answer."

"Does that sound like a kid who can't read?"

"She can glean the answers from listening to what I am teaching. It's easy to conceal an inability to read that way."

"If she can't read, how does she write her answers on tests? Do you think she is faking that?"

Miss Day fell silent. My mother took my hand, and we left the classroom, heading toward the principal's office. I sat in the main area of the office while my mother made the case for advanced reading material. The next week, a banker's box of levelled reading cards appeared. Each 8.5-x-11 card had a full story on one side and comprehension questions on the other. There must have been 200 cards in that box. By the end of Grade 1, I had read every story in that box and started borrowing Grade 3-level books from the school library.

While I felt secure, successful and confident in the classroom, on the playground the situation was different. Our playground was typical of the 1970s: concrete, fences, balls, hopscotch and our imaginations. We made up games with rules that changed every day; the boys played with hockey cards, leaning them up against the wall of the school and flicking other cards at them to try to knock them down. (It was an elaborate system of card trading — you got to keep the cards you felled.)

We played all the classics — hide-and-seek, tag and red rover. I joined in as part of the whole group, completely unaware that I was a target in tag and very proud that no one could ever find me during hide-and-seek (it would take years for me to realize that nobody was looking). During recess, the kids in Grade 1 would assemble to play red rover. Captains declared themselves and built their teams from the rest of us assembled in front of them. One by one, each one of my peers was chosen for a team. I waited anxiously for my name to be called. I was excited, because I thought I was pretty good at red rover. I had played the game at summer camp. I had experienced the exhilaration of breaking through the line of little hands locked together and the laughter when I couldn't break the line and was bounced backwards onto my bottom.

But my name was never called. I stood there, confused and mute, not fully comprehending what had just happened. My peers walked away from me to begin playing, but one captain looked back at me with the snarliest grin I'd ever seen. Then he puffed his cheeks out at me and laughed. And right then, I knew my chubby little body was the reason I hadn't been picked.

In shock, I looked over to the playground supervisors. They watched the group assemble into their lines. Not one made eye contact with me. I felt my face go hot, first from embarrassment, then from anger, then from frustration as I tried to understand why I had not been picked. I turned my back to all of them, walked to the fence at the perimeter of the school property, and sat on the damp ground, my body and head turned away from everyone. I stared into the residential backyard next door and I cried. More than once, I turned my head slightly, to see through my tears, looking at my teachers and peers to see if anyone noticed. I know they did. I saw heads looking in my direction. But no one came over to see if I was OK. Not even the adults who were supposed to be supervising the schoolyard. That feeling of betrayal, of being insignificant, made me cry even harder. I cried for 30 minutes, until the bell marking the end of recess rang. As everyone started to move back into their classrooms, I walked with my head down. Inside the classroom, I avoided eye contact with anyone. I became keenly interested in the textbook in front of me. For the rest of the day, I did not speak to a soul. I'm certain my eyes were puffy and red from my grief, and I'm sure Miss Day noticed. She did nothing.

This is the day I learned that being the fat kid made me different. It didn't matter if I was one of the smartest kids in the class; the value I put in myself as an excellent student was nullified by what people saw when they looked at me. But the cruelty of others wasn't enough to put out the fire that burned inside. Instead of crawling into myself, I started to develop a deep sense of what injustice felt like. I fought back, punching a boy in the face when he wouldn't stop lifting the girls' skirts on the playground. I was angry, even at the age of seven, that he could behave that way without reprimand. If the adults around me were not going to step in, I would.

6 FOUR REASONS TO BE NICE TO THE FAT KIDS

1) Fat kids are always friends with the geeks.

Since we are equally ostracized and made fun of, it is only natural that we should form strong bonds. The fat people will eventually lose weight and, well, we all know how it turns out for the geeks. Bill Gates can tell you.

2) Fat kids make the most loyal friends.

Your skinny friends will steal your boyfriend or girlfriend. Most of the time, the fat kids won't even try. The fat kids — having been outcasts — are extremely loyal and kind. They tend to be followers more than leaders. We are the ones who go clubbing with you, watch you partying hard and dancing with all the boys and then hold your hair away from your face when you puke.

3) Fat kids can lose weight, but those who tormented us will always be recognizable.

This really does happen. Just be nice to the fat kids. You never know when you'll meet again. Chances are you'll run into one of them when you are interviewing for a job or facing a DUI charge. Heck, the fat kid might even be the doctor you are consulting for liposuction. What goes around, comes around.

4) Middle age is the great equalizer.

You can't fight 40. We all get thicker around the middle as we age. Every now and then, when I see a photo of someone who tortured me mentally all through elementary school, I am grateful for middle age. No matter who you are, aging will catch up to you. You will develop back boobs, your face will lose its elasticity and you'll discover that yoga pants aren't just for exercise. Oh, and one more thing. Fat people don't get wrinkles.

7 THE BEST FRIEND BETRAYAL

I spent my most formative years on Goldfinch Court, a busy cul-de-sac in the northern part of Toronto. The street held four rental apartment buildings, all built in the late '60s. When my parents moved in as newlyweds in 1965, the building they lived in wasn't even fully finished yet and they were the first to move in on the 12th floor. The lobby was a gorgeous space with a beautiful crystal chandelier, and a sunken seating area with burgundy velvet curtains, sofas and plush chairs that could be used for a cocktail party. That lobby was the most opulent thing that was partially mine and it became a huge play area for all the little kids who lived in the building. As I grew older, the lobby's rich colours faded and paled in comparison to the homes of the kids from private school.

Our two-bedroom apartment was enormous. My room was big enough for two dressers, a desk, a double bed and a nightstand, along with plenty of space to store my bicycle. My closet was also generous: I could easily set myself up in there with some pillows, stuffies, books and a flashlight and read quite comfortably for hours. Reading was, and still is, my pastime and my escape route, my sanctuary. I loved my room.

Our apartment door had a mail slot, the kind with two brass flaps, one that opened from the outside and one that opened from the inside. This wasn't just a mail slot — this was a primitive communications and eavesdropping device. On more than one occasion, I opened the interior flap from the safety of my apartment to listen to the fights erupting in the hallway. We had neighbours who cheated on each other, neighbours who we never saw, a neighbour right next door who beat his wife so horribly that I could hear her screaming through the wall. When I was 11, one of my mom's male friends propped open the outer slot, pushed open the inner slot and called me a cunt because I was lying about my mother not being home. For good reason, she was avoiding him.

In my building, and on the whole street, we were all children of working parents. We all appeared to be in the same income bracket. We weren't poor, but sometimes we had just barely enough for what we needed. We didn't wear clothing with labels; hand-me-downs were the norm. The languages spoken around the building were the mother tongues of countries across the ocean: Russia, Poland, Israel, Czechoslovakia. Lots of Jewish people who moved away from persecution overseas and sought the promise of a better life in Canada. Some British folks and Canadians rounded out the mix. All my peers spoke almost perfect English, but their parents spoke with heavy accents. My after-school babysitter, Grace, was from England. The neighbours across the hall, who were my mother's closest friends inside the building, were from Russia, but they also spoke Hebrew. I listened and learned, and eventually I was able to understand the basics in Russian; especially "Come here!" (hissed through the teeth) and "What?" (always said with the exasperation of a parent being pestered). Surrounded by so many different tongues, I discovered I had a knack to imitate the accents of the grown-ups, something that became a sort of party trick in high school and a shield when I wanted to pretend to be someone else. I once dated a guy for two months who thought I was a British girl named Starr.

After school and on weekends, there was a collection of kids hanging around the playground behind the building, or running around on the vast lawn in the front, or breaking the rules by playing in the ravine that runs between the two buildings at the end of the cul-de-sac. For my entire childhood, I felt like I belonged with these kids. In the winter, we played tag that spanned several floors, running and laughing through the stairwells. In the spring, we congregated in the playground, sharing a couple of swings and testing our bravado and climbing skills on the dome-shaped jungle gym. In the summer, the pool was the place to be; in the fall, it was the front lobby or the grassy field near the pool. During any season, we congregated in the lobby or hung out in each other's apartments. We tossed raisins off our balconies to watch them sink into the deep snow. We had snowball fights and made snow angels. We created our own fun every single day. I was never at a loss for something to do or someone to hang out with. I had a few really close friends, one of whom was named Zena.

Zena had short, coarse, curly strawberry blond hair. Her parents were Russian and Zena had not yet lost the accent she brought with her when they moved to Canada. Zena was a year or two older than me, but she was happy to be my friend. As pre-teens, we huddled together to laugh at people, share silly stories and avoid the parents. Zena was the person who introduced me to Wham! when one afternoon she came to my apartment, eager and excited to share her new favourite song, *Careless Whispers*. She played the cassette tape over and over for the next 45 minutes. By the end of the week, I knew every single word. She was my best friend. Zena was the first person I connected with, who was mostly like me and, unlike my peers at school, did not judge me for the lack of labels on my clothes, the whiteness of my running shoes or my parents' marital status. She always had a smile for me, some sweet Russian pastry and a new joke she had just heard. We were absolute equals in our decisions of what to do, where to hang out, what to buy at the Becker's convenience store behind the apartment building across the street.

One Saturday afternoon, I left the apartment to find some kids to hang out with. It was early November, and the air had just started to turn frosty. I wasn't wearing a coat, partly out of ignorance of the change in the weather, but mostly because I was a teenager and therefore too cool for a jacket. I found Zena just outside our building's front doors, leaning against the one of the white columns holding up the roof covering the circular driveway.

"Hey Zena," I called as I came through the building's front doors.

Zena didn't look up. Her arms were crossed in front of her body, and she was looking out into the cul-de-sac.

"What do you want?" she snapped.

"Want to hang out?" I asked.

"I am hanging out. Right here."

I decided to ignore her sarcasm. I moved past her, heading out to the sidewalk. "Come on," I said, "let's go see what's happening at the arena." Centennial Arena, down the street, is where the teens from Goldfinch hung out to skate or play hockey or just be goofy. I stopped, realizing it was too cold to walk the three blocks without a jacket. I didn't realize Zena hadn't answered.

I turned back to the building. "I'm just going to go up and get my jacket," I said.

Zena finally looked up. "Why? You don't need a coat. Your fat should be enough to keep you warm." She punctuated it with a laugh.

I stood there, staring at her in disbelief. Zena and I were both on the bulky side. It's one of the things we bonded over without having to actually acknowledge it.

"What?" she sneered. "It's not true? Look at you. You have enough layers."

"So do you," I shot back. I was trying to hold on to anger instead of pain, hoping my face wasn't betraying how deeply she had just hurt me. I walked past Zena, back into the building, back to my apartment. In the safety of my home, I went into the kitchen to find something to eat. Hidden deep in the corner cabinet, I found Halloween candy that my mother had not given out. I sat on the kitchen floor, facing the cabinet, and swallowed my betrayal and my tears with mini chocolate bars and Tootsie Rolls.

I never spoke to Zena again. Whenever I hear *Careless Whispers*, I think of her. For years, I felt the betrayal, but I now have the perspective of adulthood. Without a doubt, Zena was reflecting the criticism and hurtful words she faced at home and did the only thing she knew how to do: she took it out on me. This was behaviour I would come to recognize in so many people in my life.

8 BUBBIE YOCHVED

The Jewish culture is steeped in rich tradition. We tell the stories of our escape from slavery in Egypt, we teach our children about the horrors of the Holocaust, we bury our worry and keep a brave face when the next round of anti-Semitism rears its ugly head in the defacing of a school, a synagogue or a Jewish cemetery.

My people, we are survivors. We endure the guilt our mothers poured over us like molasses for not calling enough, or visiting enough or for not trying hard enough to make sure they have grandchildren before they die. Our families revolve around the matriarch — our grandmothers or great-grandmothers — the powerful, all-knowing, all-seeing entity known as Bubbie.

In my own family, my great-grandmother Bubbie Yochved led the charge. A formidable woman, Yochved — or Yetta as she was called by friends and family alike — was strong, with a mind of her own. She wasn't a meek old grandmother — she was our leader. She took little time to evaluate situations before she whacked you on the back of the head and called you a dope. Her kitchen was a hub of activity every Friday and every Jewish holiday. In that kitchen, Bubbie Yochved, her sister (my grandmother), and my aunt (their other sister), cooked like fiends for the family gatherings.

Every Friday, I took the bus to Bubbie Yochved's house after school where I did my homework until the rest of our family arrived for the Sabbath dinner. Her house smelled of comfort: salty chicken soup, pungent onions, and the sweet tomato and citrus of a beef brisket. I felt so safe in that house. Comfortable, unjudged, free.

I loved Fridays! It marked the end of another week, the segue into the freedom of the weekend. Usually, I had tons of homework to work on over the weekend, but the Friday before the Jewish festival of Passover was different, since it marked the start of 10 days off from school. Because I was in a private Hebrew school, this was my March break.

I was especially excited to be going to Bubbie Yochved's for Sabbath dinner because I knew her house would be filled with goodness, life and love.

When I stepped off the bus a block away that Friday before Passover, I swear I could already smell the chicken soup. In the house, the triumvirate of sisters — Yochved, my grandmother Sylvia and their sister Bernice — were laughing and gossiping in the kitchen as they prepared the Friday meal. I got my kisses and hugs and immediately went upstairs to the spare bedroom to read some comic books. I loved this room for the solid and old things it held — the double bed with the baby-blue coverlet, whose triangular patterns and decorative nubs I traced with my fingers, the dark wood dresser with a large mirror and a glass top protecting the finish of the wood, matching side tables on either side of the bed, the drawers of which held a hodge-podge of well-loved comic books. The room was large enough for all that furniture, plus a desk. All the kids in my family — my cousins — used this room for homework or sleepovers or just to hang out in.

Bubbie Yochved's house seemed like a palace even compared to the large apartment I shared with my mother. The house had a second kitchen in the basement, set up by my great-grandfather — a deeply religious man — as the Passover kitchen, completely kosher and separate from the daily-use kitchen. Only Passover food — food that is free of leaveners and prepared in cookware that is only used during Passover — was in the fridge, and the overflow of cooking from the upstairs kitchen was done in that second kitchen. The basement seemed so separate from the rest of the house. The cold and lifeless basement creeped me out so much, I wouldn't even use the bathroom down there, despite how badly I might have needed to go. Whenever I was sent down to the cold room for apples or potatoes or onions, I ran down the stairs, grabbed what I needed and got the heck out of there.

The rest of the house was always so full of life. During the high holidays — Rosh Hashanah, Yom Kippur and Passover — the entire family gathered in Bubbie Yochved's house. The dining room table was extended, and two more tables were added to form a long "L" into the living room. Our full family of great-grandparents, grandparents, parents, aunts, uncles and cousins filled the tables. We sat in the same places every year. There was as much ritual to where we sat as there was to the prayers and the reading of the Haggadah, the book that tells the story of Passover. Like all things in life, there was a hierarchy at play: the elders and the uncles near the head of the table; the younger family members at the kids' table. At 12 years old I was the second-youngest of all the kids. Year after year, we sat patiently, following the prayers, reading the stories and suffering in hunger from the tempting smells from the kitchen. We were hungry and thirsty, but piety came before potatoes in my great-grandparents' house.

Bubbie Yochved had a soft spot for Turtles chocolates — nuts and caramel wrapped in chocolate and shaped like a turtle. Her second-favourite was Almond Roca — a butter crunch toffee candy filled with and rolled in almonds. I knew exactly where the candy was because she hid it in the same place all the time: the buffet sideboard in the living room, left side, back of the top shelf. All the holiday candy was there, including the jellied, sugary fruit slices I loved.

Since the women were busy in the kitchen and no one else had arrived, I had my chance to sneak a chocolate or other sweet treat. I quietly moved down the stairs from the bedroom, trying to remember if the squeaky stair was the third or fourth from the top. I avoided the centre of both stairs, slowly putting my weight down on the outer edge. No squeaks. Once in the living room, I opened the cabinet door, holding the metal tasseled pull in my hand so it didn't clink back against the wood and alert my great-grandmother to what I was doing. I searched through the flat cellophane-wrapped boxes and canisters to find something that was already opened. The Turtles were opened, but I didn't dare touch Bubbie Yochved's favourite chocolate.

I found something that had no cellophane — a golden box of Bartons assorted bittersweet chocolates. A few chocolates were already missing and since I didn't have time to examine the contents, I picked one from its gold plastic nest that looked appealing and hoped it didn't taste gross. The ones wrapped in foil, I already knew, were the ones filled with alcohol and tasted horrible. I put the box back and pressed the door of the hutch closed. No one heard the click, so I tiptoed back up to the spare bedroom with my chocolate. I couldn't really tell what flavour I had, but it was slightly sweet, with something creamy inside. Maybe caramel. It didn't matter. I was pleased with the sweet result. I got away with it, and I only had one. I was not like my older cousin who once ate a whole box of chocolate in secret and put the empty box back in the cabinet.

I spent so much time in that house, I knew exactly where all the treats were stored. Chocolate and candies in the sideboard. Cakes wrapped up and stored in the fridge in the basement. Pre-packaged cookies on the top shelf of the cupboard next to the fridge, away from the hands of children. On rare occasions, I managed to sneak a cookie, when by some miracle all three matriarchs were out of the kitchen.

The exception to the hidden sweets were the cookies Bubbie Yochved baked. She only baked one kind: big, brown mounds of soft, but not always moist, cookies. Slightly larger than a hockey puck, shaped like a baseball mound with sugar crystals sprinkled on top, these cookies came to be known as Bubbie's Cookies. At every holiday, these cookies appeared, proudly displayed on the kitchen table. Naturally, we were not allowed to touch any until after the meal was completed, but there they sat, calling out, teasing, and smelling like family.

By the time the whole family had arrived, the stories and prayers finished, and the meal started, we were all starving. We pinched pickles from the crystal dishes on the table, we were on sugar highs from the grape juice, and we were ready to eat. Course after course was brought out to us. Chicken soup to start, with egg noodles, matzo balls and mandlen — a dry little puff of wheat that we tossed in. Then chicken fricassee — a salty stew made with bits of chicken and homemade meatballs, scooped up with broken bits of matzo crackers and, when it isn't Passover and we can eat leavened bread, torn shreds of challah. The meal continued with gefilte fish (a pressed and boiled fish patty), chicken, roast beef, sweet boiled carrots, a selection of greens. While the family ate, I caught sight of my Bubbie Yochved, leaning against the doorframe to the dining room, looking at all of us laughing, eating and drinking. I could see the gathering through her eyes — a collection of people, related by blood and marriage that started with her and my great-grandfather. The family she built and kept together.

Bubbie Yochved and her sisters worked tirelessly, serving, clearing, washing, and all after a full day of cooking. When the girls in my family were old enough, we all spent time in the kitchen, washing and drying the dishes, picking at the leftover bits on the platters, condensing leftovers onto one plate to store in the fridge downstairs. When the dining room table was littered with chocolates, plates of cookies and candies, the sisters finally sat down in the kitchen, smiling with satisfaction and tired eyes. Bubbie Yochved was the first to reach out to the last plate sitting on the kitchen table, taking a Bubbie's Cookie, her reward for keeping our family together.

The family gatherings at Bubbie Yochved's were the closest I ever got to what I believed was a normal family. There was so much light, love and laughter in that house. There were tears and fights too, but my memories from that house are mostly of being surrounded by the love of our Bubbie. When she passed away, I was devastated, but my grief never had the opportunity to fully cycle itself. On the day of her funeral, while the family gathered around her coffin in a room in the synagogue, I sat alone, away in the main sanctuary, wondering where everyone was. My mother had decided I needed to be sheltered and should not say a proper goodbye to Bubbie Yochved. I was 20.

9 THE UGLY BROWN SHOES

I have a huge daddy wound. It gapes so large that sometimes I feel like I'm being hollowed out from the inside. It keeps me awake in the wee hours of the morning.

My parents split up when I was two years old, so I don't have any deep memories of having a dad around and then suddenly not. For my entire childhood, I listened to my mother tell me over and over again that my father didn't care about me, that he never paid child support, that I was completely unimportant to him. Buried in these comments was my mother's own pain over the separation and divorce, the pain of being a single mother, the pain of watching the father of your only child be completely uninvolved in the child's life, financially and emotionally. I resented my mother for the hurtful things she said about my father.

It took my parents nine years to finally divorce after separating. I can't say they had a bitter divorce, but my mother spent a lot of time telling me that my father didn't care about me at all and was uninterested in making sure I had the things I needed.

"She needs new shoes," I once heard my mother say on the phone. "When you come to get her on Sunday, you have to take her."

My mother was making plans for what time my dad would be coming to get me for our Sunday out. I hadn't seen my dad for more than a month, since around the time of my 10th birthday. Our Sunday outings were special because they were rare, and I was excited by the thought of shopping with my dad.

"Hey Dane," he said when he came to pick me up. He looked tired, but he always looked tired with those dark circles under his eyes. That day was different. He seemed uninterested and a bit sad.

"Where are you going to take her for shoes?" my mother asked.

"I don't know, maybe that place on Bathurst Street." There was something in his voice, the way he spit out the words, that made me think he was angry and that this was something he really didn't want to do. We left the apartment and my dad's mouth looked funny, like his lips were pressed too tightly to his teeth. "Well, Dane, let's go get some shoes."

We didn't say much to each other on the drive to the shoe store. I felt like this change in mood was somehow my fault and I got sad. I waited for my dad to start telling jokes or making funny faces, like he always did, but he was just looking out the windshield, watching the cars pass by in the opposite direction up Bathurst Street. When we arrived at the shoe store, I recognized the store front. I'd seen the shoe displays in its windows twice a day on my bus ride to and from school. The shoes were always pretty, with sparkles or see-through short heels, and the running shoes were the same ones my classmates were wearing. This shoe store lived in my mind as the place where the rich kids shopped, and now my dad had brought me here! I found a pair of runners I absolutely loved: white, with accented swirls of purple, blue and pink. I begged my dad to buy these shoes for me. Fancy things were a rarity in my young life.

Instead, he picked up an ugly pair of brown, clunky, poo-coloured Adidas and asked the salesman if he had them in my size.

"What size do you need?" the salesman asked.

My dad looked down at my feet. "I have no idea."

I knew why my dad had no idea what size shoes I wear and I was embarrassed by the thought that the salesman would understand that my dad never really saw me much. But the salesman didn't even look surprised. He pulled out a metal plate for me to step on and measured my foot. He disappeared behind the burgundy curtain at the back of the store. When he reappeared with the shoes, I tried them on and winced with disappointment. They fit, but there was nothing special about them. They made me feel frumpy and uncomfortable.

"These are the ones we're buying," my dad told me. "These are the ones I'm willing to spend money on. Those other ones are too expensive."

I had no concept of what was expensive to my father, but I was devastated about not being able to choose my own shoes. I sat with the box in my lap all the way home, and realized that the special day out I was expecting had come to an abrupt end. When I got home, my mother looked at the shoes and said, "God, those are ugly. Your father clearly decided he was going to get back at me for forcing him to buy his child shoes." I had no choice but to wear them. They were the only shoes I owned that fit my growing feet.

I knew that there would be words exchanged between my parents about those shoes. I knew my mother would call my father, and she would yell, and accuse and eventually hang up on him in anger. I only once saw my parents fight. It happened in the hallway outside our apartment.

My father dropped me off back home after a Sunday out. I had no idea what started the fight, but from my room I suddenly heard raised voices — my mother's from inside the apartment, my father's from the other side of the door. Then the yelling stopped, and I heard my father yell: "Carol, you are a real cow. Mooooo. Mooooo." He continued to "moo" his way down the hall to the elevators. I was horrified that the neighbours might hear, and I feared that people would start mooing at my mother and I, just like the kids at school did when I walked by.

I didn't spend a lot of time with my father until age 15, when I moved in with him and my stepmother for a year and a half. The memories I carry of hanging out with my father as I was growing up are dichotomous: alternating funny and sad. Some of the stories I buried deep in my mind, especially the ones that disrupted my fantasy of a rewarding and loving relationship with my father. One Sunday, on a rare occasion when he actually followed through with plans, my father took me and my best friend to the zoo. We rode an elephant, fed leaves to the giraffes and had a really great day. Except that my father was more interested in making conversation with my friend than with me. She asked for something — drink, food, time to visit an exhibit — and he obliged. It felt like he was fawning over her and ignoring me. It was weird and hurtful, but I learned then that my father was better at building relationships with people he didn't have to invest in long term.

My father — to this very day — approaches every situation in life with humour. On the surface, this may seem to be an optimistic approach to life, and while I'm grateful to my father for passing the humour gene on to me, I fully recognize that for him, making jokes about death, loss of his own limb, being evicted from and forced to sell his home, and his hoarding, is a coping mechanism. If he can laugh off life, he never needs to deal with adulting. I now realize my father is — and has always been — a selfish child, incapable of living on his own. His life has been a series of bad choices and lies. I have tried to do my duty as a daughter, but you can't help someone who continually refuses the help.

10 THE BAT MITZVAH

The B'nei Mitzvah is a Jewish rite of passage. When a boy (Bar) turns 13 or a girl (Bat) turns 12, they are called to read a portion of the Torah, our holy Bible, and recite prayers in synagogue. It's a ritual that marks the shift from child to adult. My Bat Mitzvah happened in 1982.

One of the nice things about going to a private Jewish day school is that all your classmates are hitting the B'nei Mitzvah milestone at the same time. We all had after-school lessons once per week with the rabbi in our respective synagogues. We all went shopping for the dress or suit that was colour-matched to the theme of our party (mine was purple). Every single kid in my grade had a Bar or Bat Mitzvah but I cannot remember having gone to a single one. It's entirely possible that a) I wasn't invited to any at all; or b) I was invited to a few, but my mother RSVP'd "no" because one, we didn't have the money for a dress for me to wear or a gift for me to give, or two, she was not going to get up early on a Saturday morning to take me to synagogue, then drive home and back again to pick me up.

The B'nei Mitzvah is a time to celebrate with the family and friends of the newly minted teen. For the teenager, it is a time of stress — mostly about getting up in synagogue and singing your portion of the Torah in front of everyone you know and even more people that you don't. Your voice cracks, you sing out of tune, you lose your place in the Aramaic scrolls of our holy Bible. It happens to everyone. That's practically part of the ritual. When the synagogue portion is done, you feed a light lunch to everyone in attendance that day. You endure the hugs of old men you don't know and kisses from women you are not related to who want to wish you *Mazel Tov* — literally translated to "Good luck," but is euphemistically the Jewish version of "Congratulations." (Later, when you get married anywhere past the age of 30, it comes to mean, "It's about time.")

The B'nei Mitzvah day is capped with a huge party on the same night you were called to read the Torah in synagogue. There is a band, speeches and a ceremonial candle lighting where the top 12 people (or groups of people) of great significance in your life come up to the front of the reception hall to light tall, tapered candles. At my Bat Mitzvah, the following dignitaries were called to light candles with me:

My mother.

My father.

My grandparents.

My great-grandparents.

My aunts and uncles (three sets).

My cousins.

My grandparents' best friends.

My mother's best friends.

My school friends.

And I lit the last one myself.

My Bat Mitzvah was awkward, uncomfortable and full of

verifiable *What The Fuck* moments.

Let's start with my permed hair. I was in my second year as a perm girl. My mother convinced me that a permanent was the way to give my stringy, fine, mousey hair some life. It will be easy to take care of, she said. It will give my hair some body, she said. Sure, it was both those things, but it also made me look like a mini version of my mother. I swear I smelled the perm chemicals all the time. I didn't have flowing, loose curls. I had steel-wool curls that looked like a cotton ball gone bad.

My dress was not a cute pre-teen number. Most girls my age were wearing silk and taffeta, dresses with bows and big shoulders, pinched waists and pleated skirts that fell just above the knee. But I didn't get to wear a dress like that. In my mother's world, being chubby eliminated that possibility. We could have gone shopping over the border, but my mother was not willing to drive from Toronto to Buffalo to find dresses that were fashionable and flattering for larger young ladies. Instead, she managed to find me a purple polyester dress with gauzy layers that hid my bulges. "See?" she said when I put on the dress, "You look like you have some shape." My grandmother would have worn a dress like it.

I felt uncomfortable in my own skin and to make it even worse, the top of my control-top panty hose was digging into my waist. I didn't feel pretty at all, I felt unspecial and unnerved. I was on display for my mother's benefit and as the day progressed, it became clear that this day was all about her. She told everyone how much work she had done to put together this Bat Mitzvah. She complained about having to shoulder the financial burden as a single mom. She whined about what a chore it was to have to find a dress that would fit me.

I was, however, looking forward to a rare chance to see my dad. He was fun, not serious and overbearing like my mother. When my dad showed up for photos, his shirt stretched out over his expanding middle. He was wearing a sport coat that he couldn't button up to hide it. The elbows had fake leather patches. I didn't care though — I was happy to see my father. My mother was not, and she made her feelings quite clear when she argued with him in the sanctuary about how he had no right to be in any photos since he did not contribute in any way financially to my Bat Mitzvah. I just wanted her to lay off — not only was it humiliating for people to see them arguing, but after rarely seeing him, I finally had the opportunity to spend time with my dad.

After the photos, my father pulled me aside to inform me that I needed to tell my mother he would be bringing his second wife to dinner, even though she was not invited.

"She is my family," he said, "and she has every right to be here. You shouldn't have let your mother not invite her. I won't be staying tonight if she doesn't have a seat."

All I could think about was how I had no desire to have this woman — the woman with whom my father chose to go to New Orleans and Vancouver and Las Vegas with over buying me much-needed shoes that he deemed too expensive — at *my* party. Nice play from an adult: telling me I am responsible not only for hurting his wife's feelings, but for informing my mother that my father was expecting a seat and a meal for the other woman. I was sick with anxiety about how to tell my mother. It's what was on my mind as I stepped up on the stage to sing my portion from the Torah. I was so distraught, I wanted to cry. Even in the sanctuary of my synagogue, I felt self-conscious and afraid. After we were done in the sanctuary, and people were happily eating at the luncheon, I found the opportunity to share the news with my mother. She was enraged, and I shrank into the shadows as she stomped off to find my father.

During the speeches, my mother stood at the microphone to read a letter that she wrote to me, telling me how important I was to her, how I made her life so much better and how I was a wonderful person she is proud to call her daughter. If the photographer had thought to take my photo as she was speaking, I think my mouth would have been caught hanging open in shock. Even at such a young age, I knew what she was saying was bullshit. She was grandstanding, trying to make herself look like a wonderful parent, validating her role. I was beginning to realize that her perception of the world and the reality were very different. It's a trait of hers that has plagued me my whole life. The horror of her fallacy was capped off when she presented me with that letter, written out in calligraphy on parchment-style paper and framed. My mother hung that letter in my bedroom for two years, until one day, in an attempt to free myself of my mother's chokehold, I pulled it off the wall and slammed it on the floor, yelling at her about what bullshit the letter was. The glass shattered, and my mother fumed about the mess. There was no evidence of shock or heartbreak in her face.

Normally, the party after dinner, when the Bar or Bat Mitzvah child danced and hung out with friends, was the highlight of the event. The reception room where my party was being held had a long table set up to seat almost 20 school friends. During dinner, whenever I looked at that table, I felt so proud about having so many friends, but when the party portion started, I was devastated when I couldn't find anyone. By the time the music started only three or four friends were still hanging around. I was certain my peers all had quarters in their pockets and purses for the payphone so they could call their parents to come fetch them. A couple of girls were hanging out in the bathroom, giggling and preening, but everyone else had just vanished. My "friends" left without even saying goodbye.

11 SUMMER CAMP

Between the ages of eight and 14, I spent every summer at overnight camp. The camp was in Haliburton, Ontario, set on Moose Lake, a calm lake whose southern tip resembled the head and antlers of a moose. Camp Northland/B'nai Brith was located at the northern end of the lake, right where the moose's asshole would be.

I loved my time away from my mother. I had freedom, I made some new friends, and I was not under constant scrutiny. Just like at school, I still didn't have the right clothes and I was still the fat girl, but I was spending summer with a bunch of kids whom I didn't see outside of camp. This mattered to me. Everything that happened at camp, good or bad, stayed within the confines of the camp grounds. Naturally, kids being pros at sussing out the weakest link, I was subjected to teasing and harassment. I wrote letters home to my mother telling her I was having a great time because I knew that was what she wanted to hear. Being bullied at camp was better than being bullied at home. It was at camp that I learned that while kids could be proper assholes, there were always kids on the periphery who were seeking friendship. Kids like me, who were chubby, kids who came from divorced families, kids with weird haircuts or bad acne or noses that were too big for their faces. We stuck together and sought each other out every summer. I felt like every summer brought a new opportunity to re-invent myself.

At camp, I could swim, sail, water ski, and hang out in the arts and crafts building or the nature hut. There was an endless supply of diversions to move my mind away from the teasing, and none of those diversions involved food. We had three meals per day, plus an evening snack, so food was not accessible all the time. More than once, when I returned from camp, my mother would point out with glee that I had clearly lost weight, but like all her compliments it came with a backhanded insult. "I thought you would have lost a little more," she would say. When I started my second year at camp at nine years old, I had the goal of dieting, but without being in control of the food put in front of me, this was a challenge. There was not an abundance of celery to munch on. We had eggs, cereal, sliced meats, grilled cheese, spaghetti — I have no recollection of a great selection of vegetables. On Saturday nights, though, we would have chocolate-covered ice cream bars. The chocolate shell was the best part. I would crack through with my first bite, and pick off chunks of the shell around the ice cream inside. There were two flavours of ice cream to choose from: vanilla or cherry. To this day, if I come across cherry ice cream, my mind immediately goes to that sweet treat of Saturday nights.

Saturday nights were dance nights — we called them socials. I headed into the socials at a disadvantage. I didn't have the right hair, I didn't have any makeup, I didn't have narrow hips and a small butt. But what I lacked most was confidence. I went into those Saturday night dances hoping that just one boy would ask me to dance. One song, though, would be ladies' choice and we could ask a boy to dance. When I was 11, I asked a boy I was crushing on to dance with me. He looked me up and down, then laughed in my face. "Not a chance, loser. Go lose some weight." The gaggle of girls and boys nearby all laughed. I felt my cheeks burning and quickly walked out of the dance hall so I could cry in private. I would never, ever ask a boy to dance again.

Summer 1983

Despite the cool breeze coming in through the screens of our cabin, the air inside was hot and sticky. Every now and then, the air shifted, pushed around by the crosswinds caused by all the hair dryers in action. It didn't help cool us down, it just pasted the humidity to our skin. The prep in my cabin before the social was like a circus of eyeliner, lip gloss and leg warmers. The smell of hairspray mingled with Anais Anais perfume only fuelled our teenage excitement. I was already dressed and ready to go; my permed hair didn't afford me any kind of styling prep and I didn't own any makeup. I sat in the shadow of my bunk and waited for everyone else to be ready for the social.

Lana, one of the ringleaders, put a tape in her ghetto blaster. It was a brand-new tape her parents had sent her in the mail. We looked at the picture on the tape case, admiring the woman on the cover with platinum blonde hair, perfectly styled and teased, heavy eyeliner and wrists piled with bracelets. She looked so cool, and I wondered if I could get my hair to look like that. This was a singer none of us had ever heard of before, a girl named Madonna.

"Guys, you are going love this. She is, like, totally tubular," Lana said, flipping her head back to get her blonde feathered bangs out of her face.

"I'm so sure, Lana," said Cindy, who was leaning against her bunk, flipping through the pages of the latest Seventeen magazine that had arrived from her parents the day before. Lana and Cindy had a complicated friendship. They were polar opposites: Cindy had long, flowing and perfectly feathered brown hair, Lana's was short and blonde; Cindy was all things girly, Lana was more of a tomboy. They were best friends one day, then the next day they were not speaking, because one was jealous of the other. This was one of the jealous days.

We waited patiently for the first song to start, watching the ghetto blaster as the first blank bit of tape wound its way to the other side. At the first few notes from a xylophone, some of us glanced at each other, wondering what the heck this was. Then the drums started and we were pulled into the music. We were immediately in love. As we listened to the rest of the album, my cabin-mates talked about the cute boys they wanted to walk home with and whom they walked home with last week. The goal of the social for us girls was to find someone to walk us back to the cabin, hold our hand and maybe make out a little.

As they chattered, I was trying to figure out how to convince my mom to buy me this tape when I got home. I knew full well she'd tell me we couldn't afford it. I hoped that by the time I got home at the end of August, Madonna would be a big enough hit so I could tape her off the radio.

When Lana suddenly stopped the music, I knew it was time to go. I trailed at the end of the pack, watching the girls prance around with their small hips, flat butts and growing chests. Their clothes were so cool — *Flashdance* off-the-shoulder shirts, miniskirts, Tretorn sneakers. I didn't have any of that. I felt really uncomfortable in my one-piece sleeveless denim romper that was too tight at the waist. My shoes, cheap slip-ons that we bought at a discount store, were dirty and I think my feet smelled. I never really felt comfortable in what I was wearing. Things always squeezed, pinched, poked and crept. I suspected that my mother secretly bought clothing a size too small, hoping I would be motivated to fit into them. I felt so inadequate among all these girls, but still, I hoped that maybe one day, a boy would ask me to dance. That's all I wanted for now. Just a dance. Someone who was not shy about wrapping his arms around me on the dance floor in front of everyone. A walk home would be a bonus.

We heard the music from the mess hall before we even walked in. Culture Club ended and Duran Duran started. Once inside, my cabin-mates immediately hit the dance floor as a pack, dancing with each other, laughing and clapping along with the music. I watched from the side, feeling out of place and shy, but wanting to move with the music. Despite the ugly end to my dance career after the recital a year earlier, I still loved dancing and feeling the music move through me. I saw some of my other friends in another part of the mess hall and I walked over to join the collection of girls with pimply faces, plain clothes and limp hair. We knew what everyone thought about us, but when Bananarama started to play, we didn't care and danced in our own group on the dance floor. We stayed there for a few songs, and took a break after *Cheeseburger in Paradise*.

It was the same routine every Saturday night. Boys on one side, girls on the other. Small groups dancing together on the dance floor. Shy girls hoping the boys would ask them to dance. Shy boys too nervous to cross the floor. Feeling the pressure of finding someone to walk home with before the last note of the last song — always *Stairway to Heaven* — played. It's a long song, made longer by panic, desperation, hope and adolescent hormones.

When the first notes of the song started to play, I looked up across the dance floor and saw a few boys shuffling over to the girls' side of the room. As I expected, the pretty girls who were not already dancing with a boy were soon paired up with one of the popular boys. The boy wrapped his arms around the girl's waist; she draped her arms over his shoulders. I watched, a bit sad but mostly jealous, and tried not to stare. I was trying not to lose hope with every note. I turned to whisper to my friend Stacey, to ask her if she wanted to head back, but she was gone. I scanned the room behind me, looking toward the kitchen to see if she was helping prepare the ice cream snack. I didn't see her, but I hoped she wasn't on the dance floor. There was great comfort in knowing I wasn't the only one who was never asked to dance. I scanned the dance floor and watched the sea of bodies until I finally found her there. She was dancing with a boy I didn't know. I felt a cycle of emotions. I was squinting with disbelief, then frowning with betrayal. My teeth were grinding with jealousy but my heart was happy for my friend. As I watched them, I noticed a boy approaching. I didn't look directly at him. I didn't want him to see the hope in my eyes and then the hurt when he passed me by. But he stopped right in front of me. My heart pounded.

"I'm Bill," he said. "Do you want to dance?"

I couldn't believe what was happening. Bill was tall and skinny and I didn't really find him cute. I couldn't speak, so I just nodded.

We headed onto the dance floor, and I felt his hands on my hips. I put my hands on his shoulders and we started to move in an awkward shuffle, just two kids moving in a small circle. His warm breath was on my ear and was grossing me out. He smelled a bit sweaty, and his shoulders were damp. Nothing felt comfortable about this. My first dance with a boy wasn't nearly as romantic as I'd been imagining.

As the last notes played, I could feel myself tense. *Will he ask to walk me home? Will I say yes? Do I want him to walk me home?* When the lights in the mess hall brightened, Bill leaned into my ear and with moist breath whispered, "Can I walk you home?"

"Sure, OK," I said. I was trying to give Bill the impression that this was no big deal, that this happened all the time for me.

We walked hand in hand in silence towards the girls' camp. As we neared the baseball field, Bill asked me if I wanted to go to the baseball diamond.

"Why?" I asked.

"So we can talk for a bit. I'd like to know more about you."

I wasn't really feeling tingly at all with Bill, and I was a little grossed out by his head, which seemed so much smaller than his body. But he was the first boy at camp who had paid me any attention. I agreed, and we headed through the trees, out of sight of anyone else, and settled on the ground behind home plate. We sat side by side against the fence. Despite Bill's desire to get to know me, he didn't say a word. And then Bill's mouth was on mine, pushing against my lips. Shocked, I pulled away.

Bill looked confused. "Sorry, Dana, I thought you liked me," he said, looking down at his hands. "I guess I was wrong. I just really like you and I would really like to kiss you more."

For a moment, I was flattered that he knew my name. I looked at his tiny head, and he was looking out to the empty field. He looked disappointed. I didn't want to lose my chance to have a boyfriend that summer, even if it was for only a week. Unlike some of the other girls at camp who had multiple boyfriends every summer, I'd only ever kissed one other boy, my childhood best friend Bram. I was 13.

"OK. I'll let you." Something fluttered in my stomach. It wasn't a feeling of excited anticipation, this was something entirely different. Before I could acknowledge what I was feeling, Bill's lips were back on mine, and I felt his tongue pushing past my lips. I opened my mouth a little to give him access. His tongue was like a greasy piece of meat in my mouth. I didn't stop him but hoped he would give up soon. I felt Bill shift his body and then I felt him fumbling with the buttons on my romper. He pressed me back, pinning me to the fence, as he slipped his hand inside my romper and cupped my breast through my bra.

"Stop," I said, trying to push his hand away.

"Why? Don't you like me? I'm not hurting you, am I?" He hadn't pulled his hand from out of my romper.

"I do like you," I lied. "But I don't want to do this."

"Come on, just a little feel? I really want to know what you feel like. I love kissing you. Don't you want me to kiss you anymore?"

I couldn't even look at his face. I was torn between wanting to be kissed, wanting to earn girlfriend status and wanting this icky, uncomfortable feeling to stop. "Yes, I want to kiss you." I didn't really, but I reminded myself again that having a boyfriend might be my ticket to being part of the cool crowd.

We made out for a few more minutes, then I felt his hand creep back to my bra. He pulled down my bra, squeezed my breasts, rubbed them roughly. There was no pleasure in it. As he kissed me, I wondered how long I'd have to endure this until he would be my boyfriend. And then suddenly, he stopped. He stopped touching me, stopped kissing me.

"K. Goodnight," he said. He got up and walked away, back towards the boys' camp.

I was in shock. Clearly he was not going to walk me home. I was confused. I thought I did all the right things, the things you do to get a boyfriend. Maybe this is the way it goes, and tomorrow, at breakfast, he'd come over and kiss me in front of everybody. Or maybe not.

I could feel the sand from home base in my bra. I got up, dusted myself off, and walked back to my cabin, alone and disappointed that I gave up my chocolate covered cherry ice cream bar for this. Bill asked me to dance at the next social, but I knew what he really wanted. I said no.

Summer 1984 - Session I

Summer 1984 was my last summer as a camper. I spent the time daydreaming of coming back as a counsellor-in-training, or CIT, the year after. It was a big deal to be a CIT, a whole new world of freedom, responsibility and social rank. Then I would be free and in a position to make someone else's summer better. For now, I just had to get through one more summer, endure the teasing, the constant reminders from my cabin-mates that I was less than them. Just two more months as the girl with ill-fitting discount-store clothes and the bad perm.

My cabin was made up of the usual girls. Lana and Cindy were back. As were Shawna, Andrea and Terry. My friend Stacey was in my cabin, so that was a good thing. There was a girl named Beverly and she was new. I felt sorry for her, knowing full well what she would have to endure. Her curly red hair earned her the nickname Li'l Orphan Annie right from the start of the summer. I felt some relief knowing that someone else might take the brunt of the meanness this year. And then I felt horrible for feeling that relief.

Before I knew it, we were at the end of week 1, and it was social time. I got dressed quickly in a new mini-skirt and oversized off-the-shoulder sweatshirt. My thighs rubbed together and I knew by the end of the night, there would be an angry and painful rash on my inner thighs, but at that moment, I felt a little pretty. I headed out onto the porch of the cabin with my book, settling down on the top step to read while the girls fluttered around like crazy inside the cabin, teasing their hair, applying thick eyeliner and rolling down their socks. The music was drifting out the screen door — *Lucky Star, Footloose, Girls Just Want to Have Fun* — and the floor was shaking as the girls danced around, singing into their hairbrushes and curling irons. I loved the music, but neither Stacey nor I were invited into their private dance party.

This year for the Saturday night social, there were streamers hanging from the rafters. I don't know why the camp counsellors bothered. The streamers were barely visible in the dim lights. As usual, it was already hot and sticky in the building. I was optimistic this year. I had thinned out a little, my boobs had filled out and I'd been spared the pimples that had plagued a lot of the girls at school.

Stacey and I and some new campers were dancing in groups on the dance floor, letting our limbs go everywhere as we danced to the first song of the night, *Let's Go Crazy*. Also new this year were giant jugs of water, lined up on a table against the back wall, away from the dance floor. Little plastic cups were stacked neatly beside the jugs. When the song was done, I got myself a drink. As I was filling my cup, someone walked up to the jug next to me. I looked over, and smiled at the boy. He was cute. Short brown hair, with skin tanned just enough to make him look exotic.

"Hi," he said, smiling.

"Hi," I answered. *This is weird*, I thought. *A boy talking to me? At the first dance? He must be new. There is opportunity here.* "I'm Dana. What's your name?"

"I'm Scott. This is my first year here. It's a good camp, right?"

"I've been coming for six years. It's pretty good I guess," I shrugged. Despite my negative experiences, I knew the camp as a whole was a great place. Lots of activities, decent food, clean cabins. Of course, I had nothing to compare it to. "Do you like to water ski?" I asked.

"I've never done it," Scott answered.

"Well, you'll learn how."

He nodded. "OK. See you later." I watched him walk back to the boys' side of the mess hall. I felt energized by the conversation. This was a big deal for a 14-year-old.

A few songs later, I saw Scott moving across the mess hall, back toward the water jugs. He was looking over to the group of girls standing near me, clearly looking for someone. I looked away, not wanting to be caught staring, and not wanting to see who he was looking for. I was watching the DJ flip through records when I heard my name.

"Dana, would you like to dance?" I was so stunned by Scott's request, it took me ages to realize what he was saying. As my brain was processing, his face started to go red. I felt bad for taking so long to acknowledge him. I doubted if I heard him right, but I didn't want to make him ask again.

All I could do was nod and say, "OK."

We headed onto the dance floor, Culture Club playing through the speakers. We danced on and off all night, and I was having a wonderful time. When *Stairway to Heaven* started, Scott pulled me onto the dance floor, wrapped his arms around my waist and started moving. I put my arms around his neck and smiled. Finally! I was dancing with someone nice, someone I liked, someone who didn't make me feel gross. After Scott walked me back to the edge of the girls' camp, he asked if he could kiss me goodnight. I smiled and nodded, then we kissed, awkwardly, until we found how our mouths fit together. We made out for a little longer. "Goodnight," he said. "See you tomorrow."

I was grinning from ear to ear. I felt great and I bounced back to my cabin. I wanted to tell the girls in my cabin what had happened, that I too now had a boyfriend, but I didn't want them to make fun of me and ruin my happy mood. I also didn't want to jinx anything, since Scott hadn't officially asked me to go around with him. He only said *See you tomorrow*, but I was holding on to that little phrase.

The next day, the campers had some scheduled activities in the morning, but for the rest of the day we were free to pick our own activities. I saw Scott at breakfast, and he gave me a small wave. I was filled with happiness. All day long, I looked for Scott. I scanned the lake, to see if he was out there sailing, swimming or water skiing. I walked over to the fields, watching the activities there, hoping to see him. I spent some time at the tennis courts, trying to play, but every time someone walked by, I glanced over, looking to see if it was Scott.

I finally did find Scott as I walked from the tennis courts back to the girls' camp. He came over to me.

"Can I walk with you?" he asked.

"Of course you can," I answered.

We walked along the pebbled path, trees on one side of the road, wild raspberry bushes on the other. We stopped and picked some berries, eating them right off the bushes, feeling the little bursts of sour sweetness on our tongues. We talked about where we lived in the city, where we went to school, what we did when we were not in school. We talked about what Scott liked at camp and what I didn't like about it. It was easy conversation. I had never in my life felt so comfortable with someone. While I didn't yet know Scott well enough to share my feelings, I thought that maybe there was a possibility that we could be friends — or boyfriend and girlfriend — when we were back in our regular lives. From the conversations I had overheard in my cabin, that was a big no-no. For some reason, when camp ended, the relationship ended.

Scott and I continued walking, super slowly, holding hands. I saw some girls approaching from the opposite direction. Lana and some of her group. I was happy to see them. Being with Scott would give me some stature in their group, and maybe they would let me into their world. Maybe this was to be the summer when I finally got to be one of the popular girls.

As they approached, Lana looked at us holding hands. She smiled, but not in a friendly way.

"What the hell are you doing with her?" she asked Scott. "How can you even get your arms around that fat?" It took a second for my heart to break. I was speechless and thoroughly embarrassed. I was mortified, afraid that Scott would take off.

But then I heard him say, "It's easy," as he let go of my hand and wrapped both his arms around my waist, giving me a squeeze.

Lana and her friends walked away, laughing. They had succeeded in ruining a perfect day. What Scott did was the nicest thing anyone had done for me. He stuck up for me, but because he was the first guy to step up for me, it felt awkward. I didn't know what to do or say afterward. Scott took my hand, and we continued walking down the road in silence. At the girls' camp, he leaned in to kiss me, like nothing had even happened. He said *See you tomorrow* and walked away.

Scott and I spent the rest of the session — two more weeks! — going around. A legitimate couple. None of the girls in my cabin mentioned what had happened on the road. No one asked me about

Scott, and no one made fun of me about him. I had some happiness for a while, and for once, no one tried to take that away from me.

Summer 1984 - Session II

Scott went home at the end of July, but I still had the second session to get through. There were three more socials, but I wasn't as uncomfortable about them. I had found Scott, and he was so kind and thoughtful and, despite the teasing from others, he chose me. I walked around camp with a new confidence. I felt like I had earned credibility and that I was worthy of someone's attention. It was only a few weeks, with minimal alone time, but Scott did so much more for me than boost my esteem. His attention made me stand taller, and I felt like I was now less of a shell of a person. I *was* a person.

I always looked forward to second session, because it meant there were new people in camp. I had hope that maybe one of the new campers would be in my cabin and we would be friends. I knew that the start of second session also meant the impending end of summer and going home, but by the second week, I was actually ready to go home. I looked forward to sleeping in my own bed and I looked forward to starting school again.

During Saturday night socials, I no longer hid at the back of the pack, avoiding eye contact. I stood on the edge of the dance floor, sipping my water, moving and bopping with the music. I danced with the girls in my cabin, the nice ones, and I felt free to laugh. I ignored the girls who were mean to me or to others. I didn't need them anymore and I didn't want to be like them. I danced with the boys who asked me, and there were two or three of them, whose names I didn't even know.

At the second social, I danced to *Stairway to Heaven* with Tommy G., a lively and funny boy whom I'd known for five years but who had never asked me to dance. I couldn't believe my luck.

After the social, as we were walking out to the games field, Tommy and I walked into the thicker woods that started at the far end of the soccer field. We made out, tongues and lips exploring mouths and necks and ears. We kissed until the sun was gone and we opened our eyes into darkness. I was smiling, feeling giddy with adolescent arousal and bursting with happiness. When our eyes adjusted to the darkness, Tommy looked at me like he had no idea who I was.

"What's wrong?" I asked.

"Umm, nothing," he answered. "It's just, ummm, you can't tell anybody about this."

I didn't understand. "What do you mean?"

"This never happened. You can't tell anyone we made out. If anyone finds out, I'll tell them you are a liar. No one would believe you anyways."

Slowly, the fog of bliss lifted from my brain and I started to understand what he was saying. My smile vanished and I was so grateful for the dark. I could feel the tears coming to my eyes. I wanted to be strong, to not let him know that he had hurt me. He was ashamed of having fooled around with me and he made me feel ashamed for who I was. I answered with the only thing that came to my mind.

"Like the Go-Go's said, my lips are sealed."

He gave me a weird look, and I wasn't sure if he didn't understand the reference or if he thought I was just a giant loser. God knows I felt like a giant loser. Tommy shrugged and walked away, leaving me alone in the woods. I headed back to my cabin, but after about a hundred steps, I felt like I couldn't breathe. My chest hurt. I stopped, sitting down against a tree. I could feel sticky, sappy pine needles sticking to my legs, poking through my skirt. I crossed my legs, looked down at my hands and just started sobbing. I cried until the pressure in my chest was gone, until my nose was running and the top of my skirt was wet. I had a whole conversation in my head.

What is wrong with me? Why do people have to be so mean? I am going to tell everyone about what Tommy said.

No one's going to believe you.

Then I'll hang around him and act like his girlfriend so everyone will wonder.

No, you won't. That will make you look like a fool. He's popular. You are not. You are the fat girl. Why would he even go near you?

How am I going to look him in the eye and not burst into tears?

Just don't look at him. Avoid him. There are only nine days left of camp. You can avoid him easily. Or give him a dirty look that lets him know what an asshole you think he is. But he is probably too stupid to figure out what you are trying to tell him. He's the loser, not you.

If only I could have believed that.

12 GETTING CAUGHT

I don't know why I did it. Apart from not having any money, I can't say I was terribly hungry. Or maybe I was.

Hungry for attention.

Hungry to fill a void.

There is a legendary story my mother likes to tell of how when I was in Grade 1, I would sneak off the school playground at lunchtime and head over to the grocery store that was right next door to our school. I would stand at the front of the store, next to the candy dispensers and gumball machines, and look cute. I would make eye contact with the grandmothers — the Jewish bubbies — and smile. They would smile back, lean down to pinch my cheeks and hand me some pennies or a nickel for the machines. I soon learned that if I did this daily, I could collect and save enough coins to buy a full-size chocolate bar. A couple of my friends once noticed me walking back from the store, happily nibbling a Crunch bar.

"Did you buy that?" one asked.

I was proud as a peacock. "Yes, I did. The old ladies give me money and I buy treats." I saw nothing wrong with my little enterprise. I wasn't asking for money, I explained to my friends, the grandmothers just gave it to me. My friends wanted in.

To hear my mother tell the story, it made me sound like I was the Pied Piper of the school, marching through the parking lot with a line of first graders following me. In reality, I went with one friend each day, sharing the wealth, the candy and the delight of getting something for nothing. When the school got wind of what I was doing, a fence was built around the entire playground, closing off my escape route and cutting me off from my suppliers.

Five years later, I started stealing from the drugstore a couple of blocks north of my school. Across the street from the drugstore was a small burger joint, where some of my classmates would go for an after-school snack. I walked with them, parting ways at the top of the hill to cross the street for the drugstore. Inside the store, I would skulk up and down the aisles, making sure no one was around. My heart would race when I sneakily placed small pieces of candy — a roll of Life Savers, a package of Juicy Fruit — in the sleeve of my jacket. I would walk out of the store, look at my peers inside the burger joint, laughing over their fries and gravy, and move on to the bus stop a block north of the drugstore. I never took my stolen goods out of my sleeve until I was on the bus and safely on my way home.

That was my daily ritual. Every day for nearly a month, I repeated the same after-school pattern. I got stupidly bold when I decided small candy was not enough. I started pocketing chocolate bars. Then larger chocolate bars. I was nervous every time I stole, but one time, I was not as careful as I should have been.

I noticed a man watching me. I was walking in the aisle with the larger chocolate bars, and I knew he was nearby. I was watching him while trying not to watch him, and he was doing the same. The difference was that this was his job, and I was 11. When I thought I was out of his line of sight, I picked up a family-size Caramilk bar, slipped it into my sleeve, headed out the door and made for the bus stop. I had barely moved four feet outside when I felt a hand grab my arm. I looked up to see the man from the store.

"Hang on there, young lady," he said. "You need to come with me."

I felt sick and the fear in my stomach was growing, but I tried to mask that by playing the innocent.

"Why?" I asked.

"Because I saw you stealing. Come back into the store, please."

"I wasn't stealing." I started to pull away. "I have to go home."

He shook his head and pulled me back toward the store. I had no choice, I had to go with him.

I was squeezing my right sleeve closed with my hand. The chocolate bar had slipped down my arm and was now sitting in my fist. My brain was working overtime, trying to figure out how I was going to get rid of the chocolate bar, how I was going to get out of this situation, how I was going to get home without my mother knowing what had happened.

We passed through a set of swinging double doors at the back of the store and down the stairs. As we descended into the basement, I felt my heart beating against my chest. This was the most intense situation I had ever experienced and my senses were hyper-aware. I noticed the cream-coloured stucco on the walls. The hum of the fluorescent lights. The hallway with three doors, two on the left, one on the right. We went into the room on the right — a room that felt smaller than it probably was, with a desk and a few chairs.

I panicked and did what any 11-year-old would do: I tried to get out of it with a series of hasty lies.

"I can't stay here, I have dance class." "I have to go, or my mom will worry." "No, you can't call my parents. I don't know their numbers at work." "If I don't go to dance class, I'll be in really big trouble."

And finally, "Can I just give the chocolate back?"

When I realized the man was not going to just let me go, I agreed to let him contact my grandparents. I anticipated a lot less grief from them than from my mother.

My grandparents drove from the north end of the city to pick me up. They had a conversation in the room with the security guard while I stood in the hallway, leaning against the dirty basement wall, looking at the closed door. When they emerged, my grandfather wouldn't even look at me, and I could see the disappointment in my grandmother's face. We barely spoke a word on the drive to my apartment. They asked me some questions about what had happened, and I muttered that I stole a chocolate bar and got caught. They didn't need to know any more. I stared out the window for the whole 30-minute drive, dreading what would come next.

By the time we got to my apartment, my mother was already home from work. As my grandparents told her what had happened, my fear was building. *This punishment is going to be so bad*, I thought. They argued — my grandparents wanted my mother to be lenient; my mother was filled with rage at the embarrassment of the situation and felt her parents were interfering by trying to tell her what to do. I sat on our couch, looking down at my fists on my thighs, and waited for the berating to start.

"What the hell is wrong with you?" my mother yelled, after my grandparents left.

"I don't know. I'm stupid. I was hungry," I cried.

She was so angry she wasn't even looking at me. "Well, you're right. You are stupid. Now let's go. You won't listen to me, but maybe you'll listen to the police."

In silence, we drove to our divisional police station, and as my fear turned into anger. I was humiliated enough by my actions, was this really necessary?

At the police station, my mother spoke to the officer at the front desk. "My daughter was caught stealing today. I'd like you to arrest her."

The officer looked at me, my arms crossed, looking bored and angry. Tough girl.

"Ma'am, I'm not sure she's old enough to be arrested," he said.

My mother was not going to take no for an answer. "That doesn't matter. She has been stealing and that needs to be on her permanent record. She needs to understand that stealing has now messed up the rest of her life."

The officer shrugged his shoulders, told us to wait and walked through a door behind him. My mother turned to glare at me. If she were a cartoon bull, steam would have been coming out of her nose. I recognized this anger, her emotional space of being on the verge of an explosion. I decided that saying nothing was the right course of action. I knew my mother was trying to teach me a lesson, but I was starting to realize what a farce this was going to be. Once I understood that I was not old enough to be arrested, I got cocky. There was absolutely nothing the police could do.

That awareness changed how I spoke to the police officer who came to retrieve me from the lobby. We went to a small meeting room, had a brief conversation about theft, how stealing is wrong, what a permanent record meant for the rest of my life. I listened politely, nodding my head to acknowledge that I understood. I only answered with yes or no.

When the police officer delivered me back to my mother, he was shaking his head.

"You're going to be challenged by this one. She has no fear. I think she knows there is nothing we can do because of her age."

The whole drive home, I looked out the window, smiling, finally tasting victory.

Dana Goldstein

BURGERS, FRIES & MUFFINS

13 LOSING MY VIRGINITY

How many calories do you think there are in semen?

It's not a joke. I have found myself wondering that, especially when I was on a calorie-counting diet. I have also mused about how the world would be a much happier place if semen had magical ingredients to help you lose weight. I won't apologize for my mind heading into the weird gutter when it comes to the things I put in my mouth. It's OK to admit that you have thought about how much of a workout sex can be, or how your new yoga regime has increased your flexibility.

When you are a plus-size woman, sex is not always easy, or pretty, or even desirable. My husband, who at one time was over 300 pounds, is a loving, giving partner. I have no complaints. My issues in bed are mine alone — not feeling sexy when I have a horrible eating week, feeling deflated by the numbers on the scale, catching a glimpse of myself in the mirror and being disgusted with my reflection. The buzzkillers are relentless and extremely hard to put aside when you are trying to get it on. My relationship with sex is warped, having started with losing my virginity the summer I turned 15.

I loved summer. No school, longer days and no extracurricular activities. I stopped going to camp the previous summer when I decided I did not want to return as a counsellor. Summer meant I could mostly come and go as I pleased, as my mother worked all day and I was only working part-time at Canada's Wonderland as a cashier. The bulk of my time was spent at the pool and hanging out with the neighbourhood kids I'd known my whole life. I should have revelled in the freedom, but I felt disjointed and disconnected, looking for something. Somehow, I started hanging out with a crowd I'd only known peripherally. It was a small group of boys and girls whom I'd always steered clear of, having been told that they were all bad news. I knew one of the girls got pregnant at 16, a scandal that had the Russian moms clucking with pity and the Jewish moms shaking their heads in disgust. I was sad for the girl, because I really liked her and she just suddenly disappeared from the neighbourhood. I was thinking about that girl when Wade, one of the boys I barely knew, approached me.

"Hey, you want to get high?"

I knew what he was talking about, but I'd never smoked pot. I didn't want him to know that, so I shrugged my shoulders, tried to act cool and said, "Sure."

We smoked a joint, barely talking as we got high. As I sat on the grass, learning how my body and brain responded to the pot, Wade broke the silence.

"Want to have sex?"

"Ummm, sure. Where?" That would be two new experiences in one day!

"Let's go to the ravine. We can do it on the grass." Immediately, my mind went into romantic mode. I was playing a montage of every love scene from every teen movie I'd watched. It was a John Hughes montage, mostly. *Sixteen Candles. Some Kind of Wonderful. Pretty in Pink.*

Wade and I walked away from the other kids, all of who knew

where we were going and what we would be doing.

We found a spot on the grassy hill behind one of the buildings on my street. The little stones and spiky weeds dug into my ass while the boy who took my virginity grunted on top of me. We were both 15, trying to act romantic, but with no clue what that even looked like. I'd known the boy for years, the way you generally know someone who lives in your neighbourhood. We were not friends, we didn't hang out with the same people, but some of our circles overlapped. He was bad-ass and everything my parents would hate: a low-class, barely cute, non-Jew whose father was the superintendent of one of the buildings. I wish I could say I was lying.

Losing my virginity was not a great event. Maybe it was the pot, but I felt dispassionate about it. Numb. Going through the motions. Waiting for the pain of the first few thrusts to be over. When it was done, I walked across the street, back to my apartment, completely unaware that I was bleeding. My mother was on the living room couch, watching TV, a full ashtray on the side table to her left and an empty bowl beside her on the couch. I went to the bathroom and when I saw the blood, I felt nothing at all. No pain, no regret, no fear. I was no longer romantically dreaming about the life I would have with my first. I wasn't worried about the possibility of getting pregnant. I was a blank. I don't know what I was expecting, but John Hughes made a big deal about giving away your cherry. I just didn't get it.

Over the course of that summer, at least twice per week, Wade and I got high and had sex. We moved from the ravine into his bedroom in the first-floor apartment he shared with his parents and older brother. I did not enjoy one bit of it. I didn't hate it, either. I had a companion who was happy to see me (you think?) and I was living the teenage dream of a life without supervision. One afternoon, after I had just treated him to my first-ever attempt at oral sex, we were lying on his bed with our arms wrapped around each other, when he said, "I want to ask you something."

"What?" I asked.

He was thinking, not speaking.

"What?" I prompted.

"OK, so I don't usually do this with girls like you …"

I cut him off. "Girls like me?" I said. "Girls. Like. Me?" I was angry and sat up. "You mean fat girls?"

He looked shocked, like he was not anticipating the outburst. "No," he said quietly. "I meant girls I just have sex with. I *was* going to ask you to be my girlfriend, but never mind that now."

I was stunned into silence. I did not see that coming. I took a few seconds to process this: Wade could be my first real-life, not summer-camp-boyfriend. He was fun to hang out with — the sex thing might have been our only connection — but did I even really like this guy? For the first time in my 15 years, I responded with what was in my heart instead of answering with what I thought should be the right answer.

"Ummm, Wade, that's a really nice thing and I'm sorry I jumped the gun. I just assumed you were going to say 'fat girls.'"

"Geez," he said, "you've got issues. But I can work with that. I really like you."

I blushed. "Thanks, but I don't want to be your girlfriend. Can't we just be friends with benefits?"

When I looked over at him, he looked sad. "OK," he answered.

I rarely saw Wade after that night. I had made things weird.

I had to repeat that to myself. *I* had made things weird. What had started as a call for attention — which I got — and a way to fit in — which I did — became something that meant more for the guy. Never before had *I* had the upper hand in a situation; usually I was the apologetic one, taking responsibility for something I could not control. This was new, this feeling of having the power to hurt someone else's feelings.

I took that lift in confidence and promptly started sleeping with Wade's older brother. But it didn't last long. I soon became bored with everyone and everything. When high school started up again in the fall, I was a little bit wiser, a little bit more experienced and fully aware of the power of sex.

14 I'M A PROBIE NOW

My relationship with my mother turned even more sour after the summer I lost my virginity and found drugs. I felt the noose of my mother's power loosen a bit and that gave me the courage to be bold. But I also felt out of joint. I had no idea who I was or who I wanted to be.

I went to a lot of parties. I smoked a lot of drugs and dropped a lot of acid. I slept with too many guys. I looked for attention wherever I could find it. I hung out with the sons of rabbis, the daughters of bus drivers, the rich kids, the poor kids, the weightlifters, the slackers. I discovered that boys were far more interested in promiscuous me. Attention was showered on me for all the wrong reasons, but I was enjoying dropping sexual innuendos and playing games with vague promises. I threw myself — and my money — at the mercy of any guy who tossed a smile in my direction. I racked up credit card debt, trying to buy my way into the hearts of the guys I crushed on. I was a complete idiot and no one stopped me. I did not have a single boyfriend in high school, but I had lots of boys who were friends. My best friend was a guy I was secretly in love with. We did everything together and he was the first guy with whom I got seriously drunk. We never fooled around, never even talked about it. When senior prom came around and I tried to casually ask him to go with me, he told me he had already asked someone else. I was devastated.

My mother spent a lot of time in the winter and spring of the following year going through my room. She found my diary and attacked me for my emotional rantings. She challenged me to explain how I could feel my life was "sucky" after everything she had ever done for me. She screamed at me for my words of hatred and hurt aimed at her. My writing was filled with teenage angst and heartbreak, but it was also a chronicle of my new experiences. At the time, my mother was reading a book about tough love and felt that she not only had the right to go through my things, it was her parental responsibility.

She assumed my erratic behaviour and anger was due to drug use and she was determined to help me get over my addiction. She searched my room for drugs, which I never possessed, and when she found my address book, she called the parents of every one of my friends and told them not to let their children hang out with me since I was a heavy drug user and probably selling to their kids. Over the course of one afternoon, while I was getting high and having sex somewhere, my mother managed to make me even more of a social pariah, turning my school friends against me, and driving me right into the circle of teenagers she wanted me to avoid. In the hallways of school, my friends either attacked me for my mother's actions, called me horrible names, or completely refused to have anything to do with me. The only friends I had left were the potheads.

My existence for the next few months revolved around getting high, getting laid and getting out of the apartment whenever I could. My isolation and frustration caused me to lose my shit one day when my mother tried to bar my exit from the apartment. I felt my rational self separate from my enraged self and I stood there, demanding that she move away from the door. She refused again and again, telling me I needed help and I needed to kick my addiction.

"What I needed," I hissed, "was to get out of that apartment, to be with the only people I had left who didn't betray me, make fun of me, or try to constrain me."

My anger took over, and I turned away from her, stormed into the kitchen, grabbed a steak knife and threatened to stab her if she did not move away from the door. I was yelling - screeching, actually - and for a second, I saw fear in her eyes. From her narrow perspective, my behaviour was triggered by drugs and had nothing to do with her actions. She moved away from the door. I tossed the knife into the living room behind me, turned the lock, whipped open the door and slammed it on my way out.

I took a bus to the only place I thought I could go: my father's house. He was surprised to see me, caught completely off-guard by my arrival and confused about what to do. He called my mother, and without arguing with her, arranged to bring me to the apartment so I could collect some clothes and other things I needed. While at my mother's, I did not look at her or speak to her. I silently packed a few garbage bags, feeling my mother's tension at my back. She was ready to spring into action to rip anything from my hands that she felt was not mine to take: a piece of jewellery, some trinkets, a clock radio. I was shaking with anticipation. This was the first time since summer camp that I had lived apart from my mother.

Later that week, my father and I were sitting on the couch, watching TV when the doorbell rang. My dad answered the door, and from the living room, I could hear the voices.

"Good evening," a male voice said, "I'm looking for Dana Bornstein."

"Dane?' my dad called over his shoulder. "Can you come here?"

My heart skipped a beat. The voice at the door was not familiar and sounded official. As I approached the front door, I could see dark blue pants, black boots, and a light blue shirt with a badge on the left shoulder — the police uniform.

"Are you Dana?" the officer asked.

"Yes," I whispered.

"You've been served," he said as he handed me an 8 ½ x 11 brown envelope.

"Umm, what?" I stammered as I reached out for the envelope.

Once I had the envelope in my hand, the police officer told us to have a nice day and went down our front steps into his cruiser.

I stepped away from the door as my father closed it.

"What the hell, Dana?" he said. When I looked at him, I could see he was exasperated. Like me, he thought some stupid teenage antics had finally caught up with me.

"I have no idea what this is about, Dad. Really."

I opened the envelope, took out the papers inside and just looked at them. My 15-year-old mind couldn't process what I was reading, and the legal jargon was overwhelming. I passed the papers to my father, who scanned the documents, flipping pages back and forth, as if he was looking for something.

"I don't believe it," he said, shaking his head. "That woman has lost her mind. Dana, your mother is charging you with assault. We have to go to court. Jesus fucking Christ."

My father already knew the story about the knife. I filled him in on all the other things my mother had done — the snooping, calling my friend's parents, the total disregard for anything important in my life — and he understood that I had snapped. My mother had provoked anger in my father too when they were married. I had an unexpected ally.

My father took care of hiring a lawyer — the same lawyer who handled his divorce. I met the lawyer on my appearance date in provincial district court, where he asked me for the short version of what happened. I could not wrap my head around what was happening to me. I was surrounded by criminals, people with whom I had nothing in common. My lawyer tried to assure me the judge would either throw my case out or give me community service. Nothing to worry about, he said. When my case was called, I pled guilty, ready to explain what happened. But the judge didn't want to hear what I had to say. He lectured me on appropriate behaviour, respecting my parents, and the bleak future I faced if I continued on my current path. With a smack of his gavel, the judge put me on probation for a year.

Every couple of months, I visited my probation officer to report that yes, I was working part time. Yes, I was going to school every day, and, sure, my grades were stable. No, I wasn't taking any drugs (a lie), and yes, I was trying to find a more suitable group of friends (a lie). Of course I felt comfortable living at my dad's house (100% true). Lies my probation officer had heard a million times, but this chubby teenager sitting in front of him didn't seem to be much of an issue. He was uninterested in digging deep, and after 5 visits, my probation officer released me from having to make my 6th and final visit.

I loved living with my dad. He was completely inexperienced in any kind of parenting, and was unprepared for a teenager. His inability to be my parent was frustrating for him, but a boon for a wild teen. Moving in with my father and my stepmother meant I had to sleep on the couch for a few months until they found the time to clean out the second bedroom in their small bungalow. But I had no curfew, no rules and no one to answer to. No family dinners at the table, lots of take out and school-bought breakfasts and lunches. I lived in a fog of high school drugs, junk food and careless sex for 14 months. I pushed all the limits and my dad finally lost his shit on me after I fought with my stepmother. I'm not sure what triggered his anger, but I find myself with my face pinned against the dining room door, my right arm twisted up behind my back while he screams in my ear. I left the next day to move in with my grandmother, but she was ill-equipped to cope with a teenager who would come home at all hours of the night and morning, totally incoherent and unrecognizable to her. I reluctantly moved back in with mother and tried to build a normal relationship with her.

I was shocked when my mother offered to pay for a 16th birthday night out with some of my friends. I still have no idea why she suddenly decided that she wanted to do something nice for me. The price could not have been easy to swallow, and I was certainly not used to my mother handing over cash. I was thrilled and planned a night at Second City comedy club and a birthday dinner after the show. I invited 7 of my friends, Stacey among them.

In 1986, Second City improv theatre was still a popular night out. The television arm, SCTV was off the air, but the live venue continued to thrive. We laughed hard during the show, and I was enamored with the funny-as-heck redhead who stole the show for me. He was cute, and I started crushing. After the show, we walked across the street for dinner, a choice I made simply for the geography. When I made the reservation, I had no idea that the place was a favourite for the Second City cast to eat and unwind after the show.

By the time the cast walked in, we were fed, and somewhat drunk. I had convinced the waiter that I was celebrating my 18th birthday and he never questioned me or my friends. I watched the redhead take a seat at the bar with the other cast members and tried to hide my excitement. Did I have the nerve to approach him? Hell no. But I was emboldened by alcohol, encouraged by my friends, and wanted to show my appreciation for making me laugh. I summoned our waiter and told him I wanted to by the man a drink.

"Just tell him I said thanks for a great show," I instructed.

The waiter had a conversation with the bartender, waited for a few minutes, and then took a drink over to the redhead. I looked at my empty dessert plate in front of me, my cheeks burning with embarrassment. From my peripheral vision, I saw the redhead turn in his bar stool. I glanced over in his direction, made quick eye contact, and he raised the glass to me and smiled, mouthing thank you. He never came over to the table of rowdy teenagers and I was grateful for that. I wasn't interested in a real conversation. The fantasy inside my head was way better. On our way home, I crossed the street the find the redhead's headshot on the poster outside the theatre. I wanted to remember his name: Mike Myers.

The next morning, my mother was on the phone, finding out how she could report a restaurant that served alcohol to a bunch of minors. She called the restaurant to yell at the manager and she called some of my friends' parents to report how I had let their children get drunk. Once again, I was a social pariah. I was a poor, portly, pothead whose sole focus in high school was to just be noticed. I should have gone for academic recognition, not the kind of recognition that goes with the principal kindly asking you to switch schools.

I switched schools for my final year of high school, and fell right in with the potheads again. I have very little recollection of being in classes during that final year. My grades were dismal. I'd gone from a straight A student to barely passing.

Not going to university was not an option in my family. It's a miracle I graduated from high school, but it's an even bigger miracle that I earned admission into university. I applied to three universities, wrote letters explaining — truthfully — why my grades had changed so dramatically. I wrote about my unstable home life, my drug-hazed high school life, and my desire to change the course of my life through a post-secondary education. I was candid in my letter.

"I'm not sure I will be an asset to your university," I wrote, "but I am ready to work. I need to learn again and be excited about the world out there."

15 MUFFIN TOPS

The essay that accompanied my application worked. I was accepted into two of the three schools to which I applied. I chose the University of Toronto, mostly because nobody I knew was going to be there. I finally accepted that I needed to step away from the circles I was in and find a new source of friends. Friends who didn't get high, or have reckless sex, or turn mean for kicks.

I loved the freedom of being on a large university campus. The University of Toronto's St. George campus in downtown Toronto was split into seven colleges — all of which provided a home base for students. You could choose your college based on your desired area of study, your creative or academic leaning, your politics, your existing social network or just roll the dice and randomly choose. Each college sponsored a program within the arts and sciences; your home college was often tied to your major: my choice was Innis College, home to the Cinema Studies program. Whatever college you claimed, you could be sure that each one had a café or dining room selling muffins with really big tops. There was little café tucked in down the street from Innis College that served a banana muffin with which I completely fell in love. This muffin became a ritual for me, my second breakfast. For me, university life was not filled with parties or dorm life. It was filled with fear, freedom and food.

These muffins were the perfect blend of banana and whole wheat flour. I can still taste the sweetness of the brown sugar and the creamy banana. The muffin tops were huge and crispy along the edges, exactly the way I like them. The muffin was not greasy, like so many muffins are, being overloaded with butter. It was full of flavour, and I had one every morning with a cup of coffee. Eating the muffin was a ritual: I separated the top from the bottom, letting the steam from the bottom half waft into my smell zone. I peeled the paper wrapping away from the bottom, examining it for any traces of crispy banana that might be stuck there. I broke the muffin into pieces, savouring each bite, eating slowly, washing it down with coffee. I saved the muffin top for last, since that was my favourite part. Most days, eating this muffin was a slightly religious experience.

After almost three years of praying to the muffin god, you would think the owner of the place would know my name, but I wasn't the chattiest person. I preferred to blend into the background. That's typical for me. I like that university let me be mostly invisible. I thought it would give me the focus I needed to get my academics back on track after being sidetracked by drugs and a bad group of friends. Not living in residence was not my choice. I really wanted to experience campus life to its fullest, but when I tried to discuss the issue with my mother, she shut me down before I could even have a conversation about it.

"I can't afford to pay for that and I'm not helping you. You're on your own. Do you think it will be easy to pay for everything yourself? Besides, they only give student housing to students who don't live in the city." That was her only input on the matter. I lived at home during my university years, always wondering what life was like for the students in residence.

I had already applied to OSAP — the Ontario Student Assistance Plan — and had been granted loans to cover my tuition and books. I never even bothered to investigate what my options were. I started university before websites existed and before I could

Google "How much is U of T residence?" It took a lot of effort to find information in those days. But the fear my mother instilled in me, the doubt she planted, made me idle. I didn't bother to find out if residence was a viable and affordable option. At 18, I was too meek, too overwhelmed and too insecure to take any kind of leap. In hindsight, I could have applied to residence, could have secured further assisted funding and maintained a typical college lifestyle with a part-time job. The end result of not being committed to university life was that I didn't feel like I fit in. I didn't try to make any close friends.

I struggled with the transition from high school to university. My shyness was a shield, the product of 18 years of being shot down, judged, made fun of, teased and tormented, all because of my weight. I know I was putting on airs and judged to be a snob. Unlike high school, university had no group projects, no hallways where kids congregated. There were college lounges where students collected to smoke and play cribbage. I once smiled at the group who played cribbage every day in the Innis lounge, but I lacked the confidence to approach them and ask to be taught how to play. I watched from the comfort of one of the lounge's couches and never took the risk. I kept myself occupied and un-alone with snacks, cigarettes and coffee.

I tried to navigate my way through the campus: I did some writing for the U of T paper, The Varsity; I served some time on the Cinema Studies Student Union, hoping that I could connect with some fellow cinema studies majors, but the office was tucked away in an attic room in the college, and no one had any idea it was even in the building. I sat there with a phone that never rang, alone, studying between classes and hiding from the eyes of others who I felt were judging me for eating that bag of chips.

I was completely unprepared for the freedom offered by university. I lacked the discipline to do the work and I didn't recognize my isolation. I can't say I was depressed, not clinically anyways. I was unfocused, searching for that picturesque version of university where the students have the perfect balance of academic and social life. I nearly failed my first year and had to really work hard for the next three years to graduate with an acceptable grade point average. I remember some classes, I remember the loneliness and I remember graduation. But my best memory of university was that banana muffin.

16 THE HISTORY OF EXERCISE

I didn't discover gyms until my second year in university. I knew there was a gym somewhere on campus, but I had zero interest in trying to find it. Gyms made me think of the over-developed knuckleheads in high school who slowed down at every reflective surface so they could flex and give themselves a nod of approval.

I did however, join my first gym at the shopping mall where I held a part-time job in an office supply store. It was also easily accessible via the subway. My plan was to go at least three times per week. When I first joined the gym, I was assigned a personal trainer who spent an hour with me, showing me how to use the machines, teaching me how to log and monitor my progress, and set some general goals and timelines. I started with gusto, diligently working my circuit of cardio-weights-cardio, tracking my progress, increasing my reps. And I watched the scale climb.

When I stopped going to the gym and cancelled my membership, my personal trainer — whom I had not seen for four months — called me for a check-in. He pressured me to sign up for extra personal training sessions, then berated me when I said I couldn't afford it and was frustrated with the weight gain. "Fine, be fat forever, then," he said.

The next personal trainer wouldn't even work with me unless I committed to hiring her for a minimum of three hours per week. I wasn't being cheap, I truly could not afford to fork out $600 per month. When I told her that, she shrugged her shoulders and never spoke to me again.

Over and over again, I've tried working with personal trainers, and it always ends in a brutal breakup. Nowhere in my horoscope has it ever said, "Chubby Aquarius not compatible with: gym rats, fitness types, burpee zealots and step classes." If I had been forewarned, I could have avoided some heartbreak. I've had trainers who see a scale that doesn't move or a tape measure that is not showing immediate results and they worry about how it will make *them* look. Some of us need more time to see the scale budge or to melt away layers of fat.

In my entire life, I only had one trainer who never gave up on me. Her name was Jocelyn, and she spearheaded a group training session in the building I was living in. Jocelyn was the most buff woman I had ever met. Her arms were chiseled; her legs were short and meaty with muscle; she had swimmer's shoulders and a wide back. Jocelyn was short, 5-foot-3, and thick. Muscle like you would see on a body builder. She wore little Richard Simmons shorts and a leotard top that showed every muscle in her chest. She was power. She was no bullshit. She was loud and forceful. And she was the best trainer I ever had.

Jocelyn had a way to make us understand and listen to our bodies, lessons that I still carry with me. She encouraged us to set our own limits and push without pain. To this day, when I do crunches, I hear Jocelyn telling me to visualize my abs like a sponge squeezing out water, and to keep squeezing until I felt like all the water was out. She taught me how to use my body weight to exercise anytime, anywhere. Not so ground-breaking now, but in 1994, no one was doing this.

I wouldn't step foot in a gym again for another six years after my time with Jocelyn ended. That's when I began to spend my Saturday nights at the gym, working out the fact that I had a boyfriend who really didn't want to spend time with me.

17 ITALY

I am not a foodie. I love food and I love to eat, but I think an $85 four-ounce steak is unnecessary and not any better than the $15 steak I can cook myself at home. I'm the kind of person who will mix fancy with practical by ordering a pumpkin and squash salad glazed with a house-made mustard vinaigrette and add pork belly as my protein. I can appreciate why people like caviar on their crackers, but I'll reach for the Nutella first. I did not grow up with great culinary experiences. Outside of Bubbie Yochved's kitchen, my grandmother hated cooking and was a horrible cook. She passed on the lack of culinary skills to my mother, who raised me on a limited selection of overcooked vegetables, extremely well-done meats, and canned or frozen foods. Food, albeit the wrong kind — fake flavours in potato chips, waxy textures in chocolate bars and sodium comas induced by take-out burgers — has played a starring role in my life.

It wasn't until university — 1991 to be exact — that I began to appreciate that food did not have to be fast, or plain or crap. That was the summer I spent living in Italy, and it was the summer I discovered what real food tasted like. For the first time in my life, food was social and shared, not solitary and hidden. I took the time to savour what was on my plate. I was retraining my palate to appreciate fresh herbs, hand-pressed pasta and veal that melted in my mouth. I ate in places that left their mark on me, met people who were not chefs, but who cooked for a living because they loved the experience of watching people celebrate the humble act of eating and drinking. It's not a cliché: Italy is as much about the history as it is about the gastronomy. I still dream of the pizza, pasta and gelato I ate more than 25 years ago, and my taste buds are still activated by the memories.

When I first stepped off the train from the airport and into the vast foreignness of Rome's Termini Station, I had no inkling of the impact this adventure would have on my life. It wasn't my first time travelling to Italy, but it was my first solo adventure. I was heading to the University of Siena to study the Italian language for the summer. I would be earning credit toward my university degree, and living in the university dorm with a randomly selected roommate: a girl named Brenda who was taking Italian history.

I was grateful to the woman from Sicily whom I met on the plane, who connected me with a gentleman from Rome who agreed to help me find my hotel in the ancient city. He guided me through the busy Termini Station, which really is like it appears in the movies — busy, steamy, stinky and clearly not in Canada. The musical Italian language bounced off the glass canopies over the trains. People were sitting at little bistro tables roped off in what appeared to be random areas of the station. The whole station had an atmosphere of organized chaos. I had never seen anything like it. Cigarette smoke mingled with the steam coming from the trains. Rows of trains as far as I could see, like I was looking into an image mirrored into mirrors forever. I was so overwhelmed by the language and life around me that I didn't even notice when the atrium seamlessly transitioned from indoors to outdoors. I passed shops. I smelled pastries and coffee. Then I smelled exhaust and the slightly sickly smell of sewage. I stopped to absorb where I was, but the gentleman who was taking me to my hotel gestured for me to hurry up.

"Andiamo," he said, "Presto." *Let's go. Hurry.*

I spoke almost no Italian, apart from the perfunctory phrases I knew from my textbook. *Quanto costa? Non c'e male. Buongiorno. Dove vai? Grazie. How much? Not bad. Hello. Where are you going? Thank you.* Not exactly conversation starters.

I blindly followed the man, and I was starting to get a bit anxious. It was getting late, I'd been travelling for 12 hours, I had no idea where I was going, my luggage was heavy, I was exhausted and starting to feel the emotional strain of being alone. The area around Termini Station is dirty and litter-filled, the walls of the buildings stained with the black soot of city life, and the June humidity was starting to stick to me. We walked so fast, I couldn't even absorb the fact that I was in Rome. Rome! The man stopped suddenly, pointed into an alcove and motioned for me to go up the stairs that disappeared just inside the entrance. Then he was gone.

I stepped out from the alcove, looking for a sign on the front of the two-storey building. Seeing no indication that this was a hotel, I stood on the sidewalk, not sure what to do. I looked around for some help, hoping for a police officer or a friendly looking woman, but the street was almost abandoned. It didn't really matter since I was afraid to ask a stranger — who spoke a language I didn't understand, and who may take advantage of a young tourist who was completely alone — for help. I went back into the alcove, noticing the garbage on the floor and on the stairs. This was not how I pictured Italy. Where were the cafés with the old men sitting outside sipping cappuccino? I did not see any glamourous women, wearing the latest fashion, turning heads with every step. I saw the ruins of Rome, but not the kind you book a tour to see. To my right, there was an elevator cage that I had no idea how to operate. I opened the gate, the metal screeching. It smelled like urine and I couldn't pull the gate closed. I had no choice but to walk up the trash-strewn stairs, dragging my wheel-less luggage behind me. I rested on the landing before the turn, before climbing the last flight.

There was only one door in front of me. It didn't look like the entrance to any hotel I was used to. The clear glass door gave me a full view down the corridor on the other side — a long hallway with curtains covering eight doorways, four on either side. Was this for real? Despite the jet lag, I put the pieces together. I couldn't fucking believe what I was seeing. I didn't speak Italian, I didn't have a map, I didn't know where to go. All I knew for sure was that the man from the plane had dropped me off at a brothel.

My heart pounded inside my chest and I stood in front of the door. I had only one choice. I pushed the door open. There must have been a bell or a buzzer on the inside that was triggered when I opened the door. As I walked in, a few women popped their heads out from behind their curtains, gave me a quick once-over and then disappeared. I turned my head to the left, and saw a young man sitting behind a desk. He was close to my age and he said something to me in Italian.

"English?" I asked.

"No," he answered.

"Please help me," I carried on anyways. "I'm looking for my hotel." I showed him my printed reservation with the name and address of my hotel.

He took the paper, glanced at it and shrugged, handing it back to me. He was not going to help me. He was uninterested in my welfare. I was not his problem. I had no idea how to get back to Termini Station and maybe find some help there. I was completely alone and lost in Rome and standing in a brothel. I was exhausted and scared. I burst into tears.

"Please," I begged. "Help."

There was a moment when I could see the young man was deciding whether to help or not. Then he stood up from his chair, took the paper from my hand, pulled out a book of maps and looked up the street for my hotel. I wiped my face, trying to contain myself. He looked at the map, looked at the address on the paper, then looked up at me with a slight smile. He pointed to the window behind him, a window I hadn't noticed was wide open, its shutters framing the night lights of Rome. He pointed again. It wasn't Rome I saw, but the small neon sign with the name of my hotel burning like a beacon. I looked at the young man with shock, and then he started to laugh. My hotel was two buildings over. *"Grazie,"* I said.

I headed back down to the street, walked briskly to my hotel and with relief, opened the doors to the lobby to find the desk clerk smiling and happy to see me. He had no idea how happy I was to be there.

I called my mother. As I told her the story about how a stranger took me to a brothel, the phone line went dead. It took 20 minutes before I could reach her again, and when I did, she was freaking out. I assured her that I was in the right hotel, perfectly fine and would just have a shower and head to sleep. Truth is, my adrenaline was pumping so hard, I couldn't settle. I had mixed emotions: fear, anticipation, exhaustion, excitement. It was dark, and the ordeal I had just experienced made me worried about leaving the room. But I was starving, so I headed down to the lobby to ask the clerk where I could get something small to eat. Somewhere close. He tried to explain how to find a good place for some pizza, but the directions were lost in translation. I think he sensed my hesitation, because he stopped mid-sentence.

"Aspetta." *Wait*, he said, holding a finger up. He came out from behind the desk and walked out the front door. I waited in the lobby, sitting down in one of the two curved back, wide-bottomed, and surprisingly comfortable armchairs. A few minutes later, the clerk returned, carrying something wrapped in brown paper and a Coke.

He handed both to me. "*Panino*. Sandwich. *Vai. Buona note.*" He gestured towards the elevator, *go*, waving me back to my room for the night.

In my room, I held off on taking a shower. I sat on my bed, unwrapped my sandwich and took my first bite of authentic Italian food. I could taste butter, tomatoes, and some kind of thin, salty and chewy meat. I hated it. I pulled the meat out — prosciutto — and ate the bread and tomato sandwich. I would never develop a taste for wild boar, no matter how many ways I tried it.

I laid in the bed, staring at the ceiling, listening to the night noises of Rome. It sounded like Toronto, save for the buzz of Vespas and the lack of English. I finally started to drift off, but my sleep was uncomfortable and restless.

When I got up the next morning, I'd slept late and missed the hotel breakfast. I was hungry, and would have to find my way around Rome for someplace to eat before check out. I quickly showered and packed up my toiletries and the clothes I wore for more than 15 hours the day before. I headed down to the front desk, and the same gentleman from last night was sitting behind the desk.

"*Buon giorno!*" he said with a smile. "How was sleep?"

I was thrilled my host spoke some English. "Good, *grazie*. Is there somewhere close I can find food?"

"*Va, entrare,*" he said, pointing to the small dining room just behind the desk. "I see you not here *questa mattina*, so I put a plate away." He came out from behind the desk, gesturing for me to follow him, then he disappeared behind a door at the far end of the room.

The dining room had three round tables, each with a white tablecloth and four white iron chairs. The walls were covered in a light blue- and gold-flecked wallpaper. It felt like a pretty little bistro hidden among the soot of Rome. I was in love. My host, whose name I didn't know and didn't think to ask, emerged from the back with a tray of cheese, pastries and fruit. In his left hand, he held a small coffee cup, and I could smell the richness of the coffee in the steam. I sat alone, filled with gratitude for one man's kindness and caring. My host (who very likely owned the hotel) didn't know it, but he was responsible for dampening my anxiety and fear and kindling my love for Italy. The coffee was sharp and hard, with no milk or sugar, not even close to what I was used to. The pastry was light and flaky, a bit sweet, and I realized that holding pastry in my mouth and then sipping coffee made for a rich experience.

Later that afternoon, I met a lot of fellow University of Toronto students on the platform at Termini Station, and we rode the train to Siena with excitement. I was absolutely devoid of the fear from the night before. The three-hour train ride took us north, out of the city, past small villages and farmland through the Tuscan hills, stopping at Florence where we transferred onto a bus that headed southwest to Siena. When we arrived at our dorm building, buried in the maze of the narrow streets of Siena, I was less than impressed. I was expecting a grand, European architectural marvel, not a simple building attached to every other building on the block.

. But when our chaperone opened the door and we all piled into the foyer, we were looking at a vast lobby, tiled in marble with staircase at the far end of the lobby that turned and disappeared into the second floor. One by one, we were checked in, handed our keys and, in broken English, given directions to our rooms.

I walked slowly up the stairs, taking in the details of just how different this place was from everything I had ever known. The polish of the marble. The smooth, worn banister of a building that was hundreds of years old. When we reached the second floor, we emerged into the centre of the open area used as a common space. The common area was split into two: one side was home to the television and post-modern couches and chairs, upholstered in orange, yellow and red fabric. I wondered how they kept the furniture looking so fresh, despite the hundreds of asses that filled them every year. On the other side were utilitarian tables and chairs for card games or eating. Flanking the stairs we'd just climbed, to the left and right, arches framed the spaces where windows were supposed to be. The lack of windows, I would discover, didn't just let in the sweet Tuscan breeze, but also let in bats. On more than one occasion, when I returned to the dorm after an evening in the piazza, I found myself dodging the bats that darted in and out through the openings, flying around the common room. After a while, I lost my fear and adjusted to them. They were not any more of a menace than the birds that woke me up in the morning with their chatter and song.

My room was plain — two single beds, two desks, two wardrobes, white walls, tiled floor, small bathroom. My roommate Brenda had already arrived and claimed her bed, but she had also opened up the shutters of our windows. Outside my windows, the hills of Tuscany rolled on as far as I could see, in every direction, like every image you see in a postcard. The view took my breath away and I suddenly could not even believe I was there. I dropped my luggage near my wardrobe and sat on my unmade bed, just staring out the window. It was the first time in my life that I was alone in a foreign place, responsible for getting myself to class, feeding myself, learning about a culture, and travelling without a guide. I felt like I'd instantly matured.

Every morning, I walked to the university, through the cobbled streets of Siena, stopping in at the *pasticerria* for a pastry and a cappuccino. Most of my meals were eaten in the university cafeteria. I was surprised by the choices, foods I had zero experience with: *osso bucco*, *pasta e fagioli* soup, *prosciutto*, and *tiramisu*. At first, I played it safe with salad, salami and spaghetti — foods I was familiar with. But before the end of the first week, I was hungry for more. I'd met some fellow Canadian students, some who had been bold enough to communicate with the Italian students and had a list of must-try, student-friendly (i.e. cheap) places to eat. And so we ventured out in the evenings, first to the restaurant down the road, the *Pizzeria ai 4 Venti* (Four Winds), and then further into the narrow streets of Siena, to try literal holes in the wall like *Il Gallo Nero*, where we were served the best pizza I've ever eaten.

That summer, I grew bolder about what I put into my mouth, and I started to feel confident with my own decisions. I discovered that if it's not on the menu, you could still order it. Most of the places we ate in were off the beaten path, with husbands and wives at the helm. In 1991, it wasn't uncommon to be fed by a highly skilled chef running a *trattoria* where there were no tourists, and as a student living among the locals, it took little time for me to feel at home. In Florence, I ordered grilled calamari with the cream and garlic sauce that was supposed to be drizzled on a different fish from the menu. I told the waiter what I wanted, and he paused in his writing, taking a second to think, then shrugged and wrote down my order. I watched him head to the kitchen and pass through the swinging wooden door to place my order. Less than 30 seconds later, the waiter was back at my table.

"Are you sure that is what you want?" he asked.

"Yes. I know it's not on the menu. Can the chef do it?"

"*Si, signorina*, but he doesn't think it will be right."

"It will be delicious. Tell the chef I won't hold him responsible if I don't like it. But that is what I want."

"*Va bene, signorina. Tua stomaco.*" OK, miss. It's your stomach.

The waiter walked away, shaking his head.

When our food arrived, the chef came out of the kitchen, wiping his hands on a towel. He leaned against the frame of the door to the kitchen, crossed his arms, looking annoyed. He waited. As I put my fork to my plate and speared a piece of calamari, I saw him shaking his head. I think he was disgusted. I think I committed a carnal sin by asking him to put a creamy sauce on calamari. I realized he was waiting to see my reaction. He was watching my face, looking for the twitches I couldn't hide, the subtle movements that would tell him truthfully if I was happy with my meal.

If I could have seen my own face, I know this was what it would have told him:

The taste was a surprise, salty, sweet, with just the right hint of fresh garlic. The calamari held its texture, but the sauce created this incredible combination in my mouth, a feeling of comfort and ecstasy. I closed my eyes and chewed, savouring this first bite. My mouth was not sure how to manage chewing and smiling at the same time. Before I finished swallowing, my fork was already stabbing the next piece. This was the moment when I realized I would never experience food the same way ever again. This was exactly when I started to become a food snob, when I discovered that while I may not be the best cook, I could be as creative with my plates as I wanted to be, as long as the chef agreed.

When I opened my eyes, the chef was looking at me, surprised. He was still holding the towel, nervously wiping hands that were surely dry. He smacked the towel into one hand, and I could see his lips moving. I think he was swearing, like he couldn't believe this *turista* had any sense of culinary skill. He slapped a flat hand on the swinging door as he pushed into his kitchen. Less than a minute later, he was back on the dining room side of the door, dish in hand, eating what I had asked him to create. He took a bite, and I could see he was surprised too. He tilted his head to the right, lifted his fork in my direction, nodded approval and disappeared back into the kitchen.

I did something similar at *4 Venti*, but Guiseppe, who had come to know me and my friends since we dined there at least once per week, outright refused to make me *penne ai quattro formaggi con ragu*. By asking him to combine his signature four-cheese sauce with meat sauce, I was insulting him.

"Non possibile. Dai. Sei pazzo." It's not possible. No way. You're crazy.

"Guiseppe, *per favore*. It's what I want. It will be good. *Io prometto."* I promise.

He stomped back to the kitchen, yelling at his wife Julia about how crazy I was and "Can you believe what this girl wants? She is mixing the wrong things."

But I wasn't wrong. The cheesy sauce, mixed with the sweet tomato and meat sauce was the perfect combination. The sauce clung to the *penne rigate*, and the little bits of beef snuck their way into the tubes. My mouth waters every time I even think of the dish. It was that good. I never ordered anything else from *4 Venti*. And Giuseppe stayed mad at me most of that summer, angry that I was right.

18 BULIMIA

I am one of the lucky ones who moved past my eating disorder. I was sticking my fingers down my throat on and off for eight years.

Like most people who struggle with weight, I have done some stupid things to my body. In my early teens, I took appetite suppressants combined with laxatives. During university, I discovered diuretic pills. I tried fasting, but never made it past mid-morning. I've been on diets that robbed my body of protein, or carbs, or fruit. I've eaten so much cabbage that my stomach distended painfully with gas. I've loaded my gut with fibre and had blood coming out of my ass.

Nowhere, in all the diet books or the weight-loss programs I tried was there ever a discussion about balance. It was always all or nothing. My bulimia was triggered by my own lack of control in my life, and eating what I wanted and then purging was a way for me to regain control. I couldn't manage what was happening externally in the world around me, but I could make myself numb by drowning my feelings with food and then punishing myself by sticking my fingers down my throat.

I had just graduated from Ryerson University with a degree in journalism. Since Grade 9, when my teacher, Mrs. Gladstone, told me I should consider a career in writing or journalism, I'd been thinking about becoming a foreign correspondent. It was a dream that was quietly waiting for the opportunity to come to life. When I finished high school, there was no money for me to go to Carleton, home to Canada's best journalism program. My mother let me know, in no uncertain terms, that she could not help me pay for university, and I'd better think about how I was going to afford tuition and a place to live and food and books, etc. She drowned my dream in a sea of her own bitterness and jealousy, and I let her. In 1988, Ryerson was still a college, and I wanted a university degree, not a college diploma, so I went to the University of Toronto instead. In 1994, two years after I earned my bachelor's degree, I learned that Ryerson had been given university status a year earlier, would be issuing degrees, and was starting a new program for university grads. I applied without hesitation. Dream reignited.

I graduated into an economy that was not hiring. Newspapers were downsizing, magazines were keeping only a handful of editorial staff and writers. I was competing with every one of my classmates for a tiny selection of paying jobs. As the end of the academic year approached, I started to panic, afraid that I would not find any kind of job in my chosen field. I applied for every non-paid internship, every paid job at every paper in every small community in Canada, plus summer-only positions. I barged in on interviewing panels that were happening at the school, requesting an interview even though my application had already been declined. No one was biting.

I approached one of my professors, to ask if she knew anyone who was quietly hiring. I needed her help.

"I've wanted to write since the ninth grade," I told her. "I'm not looking for a guaranteed job. I'm looking for a chance to learn if Mrs. Gladstone was right. I don't want to quit before I even know." I'll never know why my professor went out on a limb for me, made some calls and landed me a summer job as a reporter at the St. Catharine's Standard. I had no interview, only the good word of a professor and my meagre portfolio of writing samples.

This was my first real job, post university degrees. I now held a bachelor of arts degree and a bachelor of applied arts degree. I felt legit. With a job. I needed to find an apartment in St. Catharine's that I could afford with my take-home pay of about $450 per week. Since I'd only be there for the summer, I needed to find someplace furnished, with parking, but also within walking distance of the newsroom. My dad volunteered to come along with me on an apartment-hunting trip.

I picked him up and we hit the Tim Hortons drive-thru. It was just past 7 a.m., and the traffic on Highway 401 was light. We were just at the very end of June, when the mornings were still cool, but the promise of summer was right around the corner. Our plan for the day was to go to St. Catharine's, grab the paper (the one I would be working for!), go through the classifieds and start driving around the city scoping out the possibilities. My dad asked me what kind of stories I'd be working on.

"I'm starting in the entertainment section. Then I'll be moved to the city desk. I'll get to submit ideas for features and learn how a daily paper works," I explained.

He nodded. "Sounds exciting."

There were not a lot of options for me in the short-term furnished rental apartment department. St. Catharine's was a blue-collar town, with the primary employer being General Motors. I had no idea what the good part of town was or if there even was a bad part of town. My father and I looked at some places, some near downtown and some out by Brock University. One place we looked at was truly a shack, a one-room storage shed with a hot plate, a curtained-off corner for a bedroom and a bathroom separated from the space with plywood. It scared the crap out of me that someone truly lived there. We looked at some other options, including a few unfurnished places that fit my budget. We found a bachelor apartment, part of a six-plex house, fully furnished with a small kitchen, an air conditioner in the only window and a bathroom with a door. The apartment was a hodgepodge of garage sale furniture, and it made me feel eclectic. It wasn't fancy, but it had everything I needed, including cable.

I signed my first short-term lease and arranged a move-in day. I only needed to bring my clothes and some books, a television, bedding and towels. It was an easy move, with a couple of boxes and suitcases. Once I unpacked, I settled on my scratchy couch, turned on the TV and enjoyed being my own boss. It was quiet, except for the hum of traffic on the nearby roads. I could walk to the newsroom, passing through downtown St. Catharine's. But for that night, my first night of adulthood, I decided to grab some groceries, watch something on my little TV, maybe look in the Yellow Pages for a video rental place and enjoy my new freedom. My own space. My own decisions. No one invading my privacy or questioning what I was doing or whom I was speaking to or where I was going. It was all me.

And that is where the problem started. It was all me.

Before the end of my second week, the solitude was getting to me. I was feeling anxious and lonely. I didn't have any friends in town. I didn't know where to go or what to do. I got up, went to work, wrote some stories, met some people for interviews, went home. I had no extracurricular activities. I wasn't a bar-fly and there was little else to do for entertainment in St. Catharine's. I hadn't even found a video rental shop.

I started filling the void with food. Chips. Ice cream. Pop Tarts. Cookies. Anything that was sweet or salty and kept me company. Soon, I had one binge so large — first a large bag of chips, then a pint of ice cream — that I could barely move from the couch. I felt nauseous and painfully bloated. I could feel my stomach pushing against my skin, like a balloon filled to capacity with water. I was starting to sweat from the discomfort. *What the hell have I done? How pathetic am I?* The thought crept into my head that the best way to deal with the physical pain was to vomit. Get it all out so I could stop feeling so crappy. I went to bathroom, got on my knees, and opened my mouth over the toilet.

I waited for that feeling of nausea to hit me again so I could contract my stomach, make myself gag and throw up. My head was starting to hurt. I could feel the fibres of my bathroom mat digging into my knees. I could feel the junk food bubbling around in my stomach. At the next wave, I gagged and tried to throw up, but nothing came out. I sat back against the shower door, pulled my knees up to my chest, and felt immense sadness. *What am I doing? I need to get this food out of me. Can I really stick my finger down my throat? Stop being a coward. Just do it, get it over with. You'll feel better — don't you always feel better after you puke? You need to remember this feeling so you never eat like that again.*

I looked at the toilet and wondered if I could really do this. The pain in my stomach was increasing and I was compelled by the need to stop it. I rocked myself onto my knees, hung my head over the toilet, opened my mouth, and stuck two fingers in. As my fingers moved closer to the back of my throat, I gagged, but nothing more happened. I felt a wave of heat come over me, and the nausea rose again. I tried again, moving my fingers farther back, down my throat, pushing my tongue down. Gag. Stomach contracts. Gag. Gurgle. Contract. I was starting to sweat. I felt an opening in my throat, so I took the opportunity and pushed my fingers further back. Suddenly, I was caught off guard, and everything I had just eaten came exploding out of my mouth and into the toilet. Before I could sit back, another wave came as my stomach contracted again. I vomited three more times until the tears were running from my eyes and there was nothing left to purge.

My nose was running with a combination of mucus and bits of food that were shoved into my nasal cavity by the force of my vomit. I used toilet paper to wipe my nose, to wipe the puke off my fingers. I needed more toilet paper to wipe what splashed back into my face. My eyes were stinging from the mascara streaking into them and down my face. The smell was so gross, there were bits of vomit sprayed onto and under the toilet seat and on the shower door. I wiped those down with toilet paper too.

When I finally stood up, I was woozy. My knees were weak. My throat burned from bile. I was surprised by my reflection in the mirror. I looked haggard, with black streaks down my face, the dark circles under my eyes darkened by the makeup that had collected there. I had bits of not-yet-digested chips stuck to my chin and cheeks, bits in my hair, even a mushy glob stuck to my left ear. I was an absolutely disgusting and smelly mess. I brushed my teeth, then washed my face. I was holding on to the sink because my legs still felt weak. I looked at myself again, and once I was cleaned up — and out — I felt better than great. I felt triumphant.

I knew I had crossed a line. I consciously made the decision that this was going to be the way I would deal with the loneliness, and then I put that into action. I could eat away my feelings, then puke out all the disappointment, anger, sadness and pain. I spent most evenings that summer with my head in the toilet. Embarrassed by the almost daily ritual, I sought out several stores where I could buy my junk food. One night, I drove to a store 30 minutes away, telling the cashier at the checkout that I was preparing for a party on the weekend, even though she did not ask.

At the time, it never occurred to me to just not eat the garbage. I didn't know how else to deal with things other than being in the cycle of binge-and-purge. In my mind, this bulimic behaviour was easier than dieting.

There are a whole bunch of lies I have been told by the people who supposedly love me. And some strangers. The lies have been more damaging than helpful. Since I could read, I've been faced with a diet mantra of some kind or another. Every time I headed to the fridge, I was faced with an array of magnets, reminding me of my weaknesses and failures. Super appropriate messaging for a kid:

A moment on the lips, forever on the hips.

Nothing tastes as good as thin feels.

Stop! Step away from the fridge.

Back then though, the messaging was passive. I could choose not to acknowledge it. And like anything that has a permanent place, over time I just stopped seeing the magnets on the fridge.

It's not what you eat, but how much.

I was once told that I could eat a doughnut every day and still lose weight. Ten doughnuts, different story. This lie was based on math: less food and more calorie burn equals weight loss. This equation left out a considering factor: quality of food. Believe me, there were days when all I ate was a plate of wings and half a bottle of vodka. I gained 20 pounds in three months. Clearly not the right diet for me.

If you exercise every day you can eat what you want.
This one was my fault entirely. I misunderstood the concept of "eat what you want." This statement applies only if you want to eat celery, salad and fish. I might have also counted the walk across the street to buy a bag of chips as daily exercise.

You'll be happier with yourself once you lose the weight.

I admit, I felt great when I was a size four. As long as I could ignore the backbiting jealously, persistent harassment and people telling me, "Don't eat that or you'll gain it all back." I never heard that as a heavy woman. Sometimes happiness *can* be found at the bottom of a bag of potato chips.

Black is slimming.
One of the biggest lies of all time.

When your black pants are size 22 and your black sweater is 2XL, you look exactly the same as if that ensemble was in purple with red polka dots. The difference is that in black you are trying to be invisible; in polka dots, you are flipping the bird.

And my personal favourite:

You'd be so pretty if you would just lose the weight.
You know, if I had a dime for every time someone said that to me, I could *buy* myself pretty.

Over the next eight years, I would tell a lot of lies — fake conversations on my cellphone with pretend people telling me what they wanted from the store, talking about my fake husband's pretend poker nights, buying ice cream for a non-existent friend who just had her wisdom teeth out. I'm telling these stories, but deep down I believed that all these people saw was a fat girl feeding herself the junk that kept her fat. No one believed the lies, but I continued with them nonetheless.

19 THE BAD BUDDY

I am impulsive. Sure, I have fear when I venture into something new, but I am driven by emotion, by the promise held in the winds of change. I take action first, and figure stuff out as I go along. When I decided to join Weight Watchers — the first time I'd been back since I was 10 — I thought this time would be different. This time, I was going to join with my fiancé, Joel, but he didn't know it yet. My plan was to surprise him by showing up at the meeting I knew he was attending and signing up myself. I wanted to show him my support for his journey, and truthfully, I had about 45 pounds to lose. I was a little worried that he might lose weight and leave me. I carried a lot of trauma around this particular program: failure, embarrassment, emotional scarring, a disgust for calorie counting, and a chorus of "Don't eat that," "Are you allowed to eat that," and "Eat more carrots" bouncing around in my head. It was not going to be easy, but I was going to be doing it with the man I loved and we could do it together.

The meetings were held on the upper floor of a small shopping mall. I walked into the mall and found the only way up to the meeting room was by stairs. Two flights, curved, with a small landing between the two sets. *Way to make us commit by presenting us with stairs before we even start.* My heart was beating hard when I got to the top, not only because of the effort, but because I was nervous about how my fiancé would react when he saw me. In my head, I played out what he might say and do. Would he hug me and be grateful that I was joining with him? Would he feel that I was invading his space, but recognize that I was trying to take care of myself while showing him support at the same time? Would he be embarrassed?

The primary desk was just inside the meeting room's double doors. Before I approached the podium, I scanned the chairs in the room and spotted the back of Joel's head. He was sitting with a co-worker, a woman I knew and liked. This was an easy meeting for them to get to since they worked in the mall. I signed up, paid my dues, collected my welcome guides, my food journal and my food points calculator. I proceeded to the scale, waited my turn in line to be weighed in. This experience was already turning out better than my last time at Weight Watchers. There was more discretion and more privacy: the scale was still visible to all, but the digital readout was hidden behind a screen placed on a table, so only the person weighing me in and I could see the numbers. When I stepped on, it wasn't as horrible as I'd imagined. 186 pounds. I was confident that I would easily be able to lose weight since I was going to be doing this with my future husband.

The room had an aisle that separated the rows of metal-framed utility chairs. I approached the row of chairs where Joel and his co-worker were sitting. When I was within his field of vision, he turned his head slightly. I had my best smile on. I was excited to see him in the middle of the day, I was happy that we had one more thing we could do together and I was envisioning my skinny self in my wedding dress. After he glanced my way, there was a pause before that moment of recognition kicked in. His head whipped back to look at me with surprise. Mission accomplished.

"What are you doing here?" he asked. For a second, he looked irritated, then corrected himself to give me a half-committed smile.

"I just joined," I said proudly. "I made arrangements with my boss. I can take a bit of a longer lunch hour on Wednesdays so I can come to these meetings. I'll tack on the extra time to the end of my shift. Now we can do this together."

"But Alana is coming with me," he said, pointing to his co-worker. Alana was older, married, with grown kids who were already out of the house. She looked happier to see me than my fiancé did. "And we may not be coming on Wednesdays every week. You know how busy my work schedule can be. You should have talked to me before you joined." I could hear it in his voice — he was pissed off that I was there. He made me feel like I was inserting myself in a part of his life where I was not welcome. Alana looked down at her hands in her lap, clearly embarrassed for me. I fought back tears, moved into the row to sit down beside Alana, and stared straight ahead, waiting for the speaker to start. Thankfully, I didn't have to wait long before we were all distracted by the engaging, energetic speaker. There was a woman at the meeting who had more than 100 pounds to lose. She was in her late 40s and seemed overwhelmed with how hard it was for her to lose weight. I had sympathy for her, but deep down I was happy that wasn't me. (Fast-forward 18 years, and that would be exactly me. Fuck.)

Thirty minutes later, when the meeting was over, I was fully committed and excited about starting the program. A rogue thought went flitting through my brain: *I'll lose the weight and then dump this jerk.* As we left the meeting room, my fiancé did not even give me a kiss. He barely even looked at me as he rushed out of the room saying, "I've got to get back to work."

"OK," I smiled back, "I'll talk to you later." On my drive back to work, I replayed the incident over and over in my head. How could he not have been happy to see me? Was I too fat? Was he trying to hide something? Did I cross some kind of line between work life and personal life? What did I do wrong?

Over the next six months, we only managed to share one more meeting together. He switched his meeting days frequently, partly driven by his work schedule and partly by his need to shut me out of that part of his life.

20 THE DRESS

At my size, dress clothes are ugly, even if you have a lot of money. Designers still think that sequined collars, drapey cardigans and flowy pants are the way to go for the round and rotund demographic. You know what? Those kind of clothes make me look ridiculous and old. I feel like a mother-of-the-bride and not in a good way. The dresses are equally hideous, with pleats — lots and lots of pleats — across the chest. To distract the eye from the girth, they say. What utter bullshit. When you are between size 20-26, there is nothing you can do to mask the weight. Sequins, pleats and other ridiculous decorations just make me look like an over-adorned cupcake with legs. Or like the fancy, frilly covers people put on turkey legs.

At the best of times, shopping for plus-size clothing is an exercise in self-hate. When you are plus size, every trip to the fitting room can set off an emotional breakdown. The feeling is something akin to trying on a swimsuit over and over and over. It probably wouldn't be so bad if the designers could agree on sizing guidelines. I acknowledge that this happens with regular-size clothing as well. I know the panic that emerges when we suddenly find ourselves upsizing for no good reason.

Let's start with the stores that claim to sell plus-size clothing, but really don't. First, there is the challenge of finding the plus section, because in this store it is usually buried behind the clearance rack. Like the company is embarrassed to sell anything larger than a 14. Well, they should be embarrassed — the 2XL barely made it over my boobs. I can't be certain what size their model was, but I would guess that she was maybe a medium with some monthly bloating.

My next favourite store is the one that carries several different lines in plus-size clothing. Someone in the corporate office decided it would be clever to size the in-house brand differently than all the other plus-size labels. I suppose someone was thinking that sales would boom when women realized they only needed a size 21 and not a 24, assuming of course they had the patience to figure out exactly how the sizing works. Believe me, after trying on four pairs of pants to find the right size, I was too exasperated to think about the smaller number. And by the way, this is the same store where you can buy a pair of blue pants in one size and then need to go two sizes larger for the same pants in black.

Next on my list is the store that has the audacity to charge a higher price for a plus size. Why on earth should I have to pay more because I want the same skirt my skinny friends bought? Because of the 14 inches of extra fabric? That's just extortion and I was already pissed off because this store parks the plus section next to the "OMG my grandma would love that sparkly sweat suit" section.

And last but not least — and this is not unique to any particular store — why is it that some designers assume that if you need a size 22, you must be six feet tall? Overweight women, myself among them, have a tendency to grow out, not up. I am tired of having to alter my clothes so that my jeans aren't dragging behind me like a wedding train.

I have to be fair though. There are a handful of stores that manage to get it right. The pants are the right length (God bless the person who came up with plus petite!), the sizes are all the same regardless of the garment colour, and they are priced fairly. There are even some stores that don't carry plus sizes, but are generous with the XXL. And that, to me, is like a lottery win.

I also know from personal experience that evening wear is much nicer when you are a rack size. I was a size 6 when I was at my thinnest, but before I reached that milestone, I was a size 12 when the corporate Christmas party season came around. I shopped for almost three months, trying on a huge variety of dresses. For the first time in my life, I was ready to dance with my hands in the air, to not give a shit if my top lifted a bit and exposed my midriff. I had a waist! I had a flat stomach! I had sex appeal! Being smaller on top made most dresses gape around my boobs, but at least I could dress my age. I finally settled on a flared skirt and matching fitted top, and I looked dynamite. That holiday season was supposed to be the celebration of a massive victory for me, but my fiancé gave my outfit, and my new sleek body, less than a passing glance. A classic case of transference, he passed all his misery onto me, trying to — and succeeding at — making me feel less-than spectacular.

Later, when it came to shopping for a dress for our engagement party, I headed to Yorkdale Shopping Centre, a high-end mall in central Toronto. As usual, the parking lot at Yorkdale was insane. I'd already circled the western side of the parking lot and had not found a free spot. Twice, I watched people walk from the mall and head toward the lot. I watched to see where they would go, then I gave my Honda CRV some gas, trying to get to the spot before someone else got there. Twice, I pulled into the aisle where I saw the person get into their car and discovered another car already there, blinker engaged. I needed to avoid starting this shopping trip frustrated from the outset. I needed to find calm, clear my head, and be zen about finding a parking spot and finding a dress. Since Joel's company Christmas party, I had lost another 12 pounds. It was not easy to get through the holidays and still lose weight. My mantra became "No, thank you." I had been working so hard, and I wasn't about to let eggnog, Christmas cookies and buttery mashed potatoes derail my efforts. Since I started Weight Watchers, I'd lost 44 pounds and I felt the best I had ever felt in my life. I was lighter, stronger and extremely proud of myself. I walked with my head held higher, there was a spring in my step and for the first time in my life, men were noticing me. But first, I needed to find a damn parking spot.

I finally found a spot in the south lot, and headed into the mall to start the search. I mentally prepared myself for an exhausting day of walking into many stores and trying on many dresses. I moved past the stores I knew didn't sell formalwear, and slowed down when I neared one of the designer stores that I had bypassed my entire shopping life, because they never carry plus sizes. This time, I paused in front of the doorway, wondering if maybe this was the day. I walked in, nervous and completely unaware of how the weight loss had changed my body shape. Within a minute, I fell in love with a gorgeous sleeveless and body-skimming dress. The dress was made of a heavy silk, a muted silver/purple colour that shifted tone depending on how the light hit the fabric. Looking at the dress sizes, I was disappointed to see that the largest was an eight.

"Would you like to try that?" the salesman asked.

"I would, but I was hoping you had a 12. This eight will never fit me."

The salesman's eyes travelled up and down my body, assessing my curves.

"Honey," he said, plucking the dress off the rack. "That eight is going to fit you. C'mon, let's try." He hung the dress in the fitting room and bowed, sweeping his arm towards the room, inviting me in.

In the dressing room, I said a short prayer to the design gods: please let this dress pass over my hips, please let the salesman not be cruel or laugh when I come out with the dress bunched up and stuck at my thighs, please let me find a dress today. To my surprise, the dress dropped over my hips and thighs with ease. There was no mirror inside the room — in this store you needed to come out of the room to see your reflection. I walked out, feeling incredibly nervous and self-conscious about how I must look, sure that the dress was revealing my cottage cheese thighs and too-generous bottom.

"Oh my God," the salesman whispered. I turned around to face the mirror. I briefly had no idea who was looking back at me. This dress was fucking perfect for me. It was loose in the right places and accentuated my curves. I could not stop looking at myself. I started to cry. This was the first time in my life that I could walk into a store and buy a dress off the regular rack. This was a huge milestone for me. I envisioned future shopping trips where I could just point to whatever I wanted because everything would fit. In that moment, I realized that the world of wedding dresses no longer had limits. Suddenly, it didn't matter what the price on this dress' tag said. I had to have that dress. Thank God for American Express. I carried that dress bag home with unbelievable pride. I couldn't wait to wear it to the party and I didn't let anyone see it until the day of.

The shindig was held in the party room of my mother's condo. My parents gushed over how beautiful I looked. My fiancé muttered how nice I looked. And then added that maybe I could lose five more pounds. He took the wind out of my sails with that one comment. He spoiled the whole night for me and made me self-conscious.

When I look at the pictures from the engagement party, all I can see are the bones sticking out on my neck, making my head look disproportionately large. Even though he ruined the party for me, he was never able to take that moment in the store away from me. I still have the dress, because despite the hurt around it, I still see it as a victory.

21 CONTAGION

My first thought that morning was "I should dump my fiancé." I ignored it because I was stuck in my apartment, in pain and alone, suffering from a horrible case of shingles on my left thigh.

I had never even heard of shingles, but I should have known something was wrong when, the week prior, the skin on my outer left thigh, down to my knee, felt tight, like something was stretching the skin to its limit. The spots — a visible symptom of shingles — did not emerge slowly. I woke up one Friday morning to a rash — not itchy yet, but burning.

At the doctor's office, I noticed the rash had gotten larger and started to itch, and the pain was unreal. I wanted to scratch, but touching the area was incredibly painful. It felt like my flesh was separating from itself. Shingles is a contagious disease, but only through direct contact with the fluid from the rash. That wasn't the only reason I shouldn't go to work, my doctor explained. I was home-bound because there was risk of infection from my pants rubbing on the rash, from not being able to let the rash breathe, and any stress might help the rash spread.

"You realize I am about to get married." I laughed. "Not much chance of avoiding stress altogether."

I was told to stay home, medicate for the pain, take oatmeal baths and wait it out. I left the office with some antibacterial ointment and a letter to my employer, explaining why I would not be at work for at least two weeks. I went home and made two phone calls: one to my employer and one to my fiancé. My boss was sympathetic, and she didn't even sound put out by having to find someone to cover my shifts for the next two weeks. I told her I'd swing by the store to drop off my doctor's note when it didn't feel like my pants were large-grain sandpaper against my leg.

"Don't worry about that. Bring it in with you when you are back at work," she told me. "Is there anything I can do to help?"

"Thank you for offering," I answered. "Joel will help me out."

I hung up and immediately called the man I was going to marry in 50 days. I left a message on his voicemail.

I was laying on my couch in my apartment, no pants on, flipping channels and smoking cigarettes. After an hour, I ran my first oatmeal bath and soaked until I felt no more pain. I found the loosest pair of shorts I had and rolled up the leg until the rash was fully exposed. Within 30 minutes, the pain started again, this time spreading from the rash and radiating around my thigh. Front to back. I took some Tylenol to quell the pain and laid down on the couch, on my right side, and willed the pain away. I was trying to doze, but the pain kept me awake. When Joel called me back three hours later, I was in tears and barely able to speak through the pain.

"I've never even heard of shingles," he said. Maybe it was because I was tired and in pain, but I swear I could hear an accusation in his voice, like he thought I was making it up.

His irritated tone snapped me out my pain and grief for a minute, long enough to tell him I couldn't put pants on and I needed groceries. I told him I couldn't stand long enough to cook dinner and I had no frozen dinners in my freezer.

"Can you make a can of tuna?" he asked.

Wow, I thought, *can you not even come take care of me a little bit?* But what I said was, "I'm not sure I even have a can of tuna. I'll check later when the Tylenol kicks in." I should have said, *Hey fucker, why don't you bring your fiancée some dinner and pick up some groceries for her*, but I held my tongue. I always tiptoed around the difficult moments, not wanting to be too demanding, afraid that I would push him away.

He sighed. "I can pick up some Swiss Chalet for you and bring it over."

I smiled to myself. Finally! He was going to buy me dinner and come keep me company. While I waited for him to come over, I wrote up my grocery list to give him, hoping he won't mind picking up some basics at the store two blocks away.

Just under an hour later, my fiancé called.

"I'm just in the parking lot," he started. "I'll bring the food up and leave it outside your door. Don't open the door until I leave. I don't want to catch your shingles."

I was in shock. Once again, he had found a way to abandon me. I felt a fist of pressure in my chest, and then I was crying. Sobbing, full on, by the time he knocked on the door and reminded me to not open it until he was out of range.

"OK," I said, unable to stop my tears. "Thanks for bringing the food." He didn't notice the change in my voice, or hear my sniffling, because he was already halfway down the hallway, heading towards the elevator.

I opened the door, to see if maybe he was waiting at the elevators so he could wave, or blow a kiss to the woman he loved, but when I looked down the hallway, the corridor was empty. The clear plastic Swiss Chalet bag sat on the floor in front of my doorway, steam already evaporating from the container of warm food. I brought it in, placed it on my coffee table and just looked at it. I started crying even more when I started to think about all the times my fiancé had let me down, left me alone or just didn't care.

I got dressed, wincing with every movement as my pants rubbed my rash. I walked, slowly, across the street to the convenience store. I was limping, my physical pain taking over as my emotional pain turned to resentment, and all I could think about was getting to the store to buy some potato chips. I bought two large bags of sour cream and onion chips, not caring that the store owner was probably mentally noting that I'd come for junk food *again*, that my hair was greasy and my eyes puffy. I returned to my apartment, put the Swiss Chalet in the fridge and blindly consumed both bags of chips.

I spent the weekend alternating between feeling sorry for myself, being disgusted with myself, being angry at myself and then switched all those feelings to my fiancé. The next day, I wrapped my leg in the gauze my doctor gave me and got some groceries to hold me for the next week. I had short conversations with my fiancé, and I hadn't asked him again to get me groceries — I was afraid he'd say no and I'd start feeling the hurt all over again. I was used to taking care of myself, of having no one to count on for my care. I got more junk food to help me ride out any heartache. I had conversations in my head, telling myself I should dump his ass and move on to find someone who treated me well. Then I heard my mother's critical voice, telling me I am impossible to live with and no one would ever want to be with me. Deep down, part of me knew I was keeping him around to defy her and prove her wrong.

I envisioned life without my fiancé, and realized it might look better than life with him. I was resolved to end our relationship, and I started rehearsing what I would say. On Monday, Day 4 of shingles, I told him I was not as contagious and he could come over on Tuesday after work. "You don't have to stay long or even sit beside me," I said. He agreed to come, and I was ready to end the garbage relationship.

But it never happened. Day 5 was September 11, 2001.

22 THE END OF THE WORLD AS I KNOW IT

Joel and I first dated, briefly, when we were in our early 20s. We met when friends of mine, one of who was Joel's cousin, invited us up to Western University for homecoming weekend. I volunteered to drive Joel out to London, Ontario, since I was the one with my own vehicle. The talk for the 90-minute drive was light and I had to work hard to get any information out of Joel. I can't say the drive was awkward, but it certainly wasn't filled with engaging conversation. That weekend, we stacked plastic shot glasses into towers and marveled at how many 99-cent shots we had downed. We laughed, we danced and we drank some more until we stumbled back to my friend's rental house. In my drunken bliss, I may have become overly affectionate with Joel, gently touching his arm, leaning into him as we walked, and giving off signals that I was ready to fool around. He never took the bait, and I remember wondering what was wrong with him. Every man I had ever met was usually responsive to any kind of sexual innuendo.

It's a thought I would have while we were dating, three years after we first met. He was working at a department store near my house and we just ran into each other. The conversation was easier than it had been that weekend in London and we were both smitten. He asked for my number and called me a couple of days later for a date. We dated for two years. We fooled around, but when it came to sex, Joel insisted he wanted to wait until he was married. I found it frustrating, and wondered how a guy in his 20s could be a virgin. It seemed weird to me, not cute, but I let it go. I had to respect his wish even if it was not aligned with any of mine. When this first round of dating came to an end and we broke up — when he

139

dumped me — I laughed when he told me it was him, not me. Somewhere in the back of my brain, my subconscious tried to tell me this was a good thing, but my conscious brain lashed out at him for being a horrible boyfriend anyways. I became belligerent, giving him shit for not being there when I needed him, for skipping my birthday because he was too tired, for making me feel like I was at the bottom of his priority list.

Seven years later, when Joel's face appeared before my cashier's window at Casino Niagara, I have to admit, my heart started beating quickly. I was happy to see him.

"I'd like to take you out to dinner," he said. "Can I have your number?" I was surprised and excited. I wrote my phone number on a scrap piece of paper, and passed it through the bottom of my window, pausing so the security camera above me could see what was leaving my hands.

He called me two days later, and we made a date for the next time I would be in Toronto. An irritation flashed through my mind: *Shouldn't he be coming to Niagara Falls to date me? Why am I making the effort to plan a trip to Toronto for a date?* I pushed the thought aside.

Nevertheless, we had an amazing time: dinner and a movie. We ended the night making out. I was floating on a romantic high when I got home. My glee was extinguished when I turned on the television to discover Princess Diana had died in a horrible car accident. I should have taken that as a sign.

We dated again, sexlessly, for three years. At some point, I stopped thinking there was something wrong with him and started wondering what was wrong with me. I bent my will to make him happy. I accommodated his wishes. I overlooked his insensitivities. I was so desperate to prove my mother wrong, to show her that I was worthy of being loved, that I willingly made myself a doormat and accepted Joel's shitty behaviour.

On our wedding day, I was the smallest I had ever been since I was a kid. My body had shrunk everywhere and my wardrobe was filled with girls' size 16 tops and women's size 6 bottoms. I felt amazing and strong in body, but beaten down and confused in mind.

I cried almost daily as soon as we were married. Our honeymoon at Club Med in Turks and Caicos was not the sex-filled, hand-holding period of intimacy I imagined. I spent a lot of my honeymoon looking out at the ocean, troubled by my husband's silence, feeling lonely and wondering if I had made a huge mistake. When we returned and settled in our condo, Joel spent his free time with his male friends while I was at work. Almost every weekend after our wedding, when most couples insulate themselves in the honeymoon phase, he had one of his friends from out of town crashing in the second bedroom of our condo. I was subjected to his hurtful comments, his lack of affection toward me, his desire to do anything but spend time with me. This was not how I pictured married life.

Emotionally, I was drained, trying to appease my husband, trying to figure out what I'd done to disappoint him. Over the course of 23 months, the list of disappointments grew. I was fired from my job and he called a female friend of his to comfort him. *He* was embarrassed that I was fired, and he hissed that at me in front of his friend. I tried to cook for him and when I burned a dish he laughed at me and told me to just stay out of the kitchen. He built a wall of pillows between us in our marriage bed and told me he was tired when I tried to climb over for some intimacy. When I started to gain weight, he asked me how I thought I could manage to be a mother when I could not even take care of myself.

I was working as a human resources manager at a retail chain, a job that entailed evening and weekend shifts. On my closing shifts, I wasn't eager to get home. My 35-minute drive from the store to our condo gave me plenty of time to think about what waited for me at home: solo time on the couch, watching late-night television and snacking on chips or chocolate. If someone could have looked inside my penthouse windows, they would have seen a sad, lonely young woman, not a happy, glowing newlywed. After almost two years of marriage, I figured I should stop waiting for the honeymoon stage to start. Every time I worked the late shift, I could be sure that my husband would be fast asleep by the time I got home. He never waited up for me and never showed any interest in talking about my day. In fact, four days could pass without us speaking to one another. He rose early, while I was still in deep sleep and I was gone long before he came home. I would call him at work just to say hi, but he never answered his phone. I left messages letting him know I was thinking about him, but that was a one-sided effort. I couldn't understand how my husband could go so many days without speaking to his wife.

One night, as I passed the dining room table in the dark, I knocked over his work bag and a small bottle fell out, rolling under the dining room table. It was a tiny bottle, with a picture of a man's flexed, muscular arm on its label. I opened the bottle and didn't even have to bring the bottle to my nose. I could already smell that it was sniffing glue. *Why the hell would my husband have sniffing glue?*

My curiosity got the better of me, and my stomach was already bubbling with anxiety when I opened the other sections of his bag. My whole body was tingling and I was having trouble breathing. I held my breath, listening to my husband's soft snoring in our bedroom. I started snooping, found his bankbook and opened it up. I was stunned at the low balance, by the negatives barely covered by his monthly — generous — paycheque. I started scanning the charges, trying to discover what he was spending his money on. And then I noticed the line items in the bankbook were peppered with debit charges from someplace unfamiliar. I headed into our spare bedroom, turned on my aging computer, my heart hammering in my chest while I waited for the computer and my Yahoo! search engine to load.

It didn't take me long to learn what The Barracks was: a seedy, let's-have-sex-in-the-corner gay bathhouse. I sat in shock at the computer, trying to process what the hell was happening. The weight of his betrayal kept me stuck in my chair, unsure of what my next move should be. I sat in front of my computer, staring at the same search results screen for almost an hour. It was the mundane habits that got me moving: *I should brush my teeth. Take off my makeup. Get into bed.* When I started brushing my teeth, the tears came, and I leaned over the sink, foamy toothpaste drippings mixing in with my tears. I cried silently, since I didn't want to wake Joel and deal with him at that moment.

All night, I tossed and turned, not sure how to handle it. When Joel got in the shower in the morning, I was awake, but pretending to sleep. I heard the shower stop and listened as he shaved then dressed. Once I heard him move into the kitchen, I pulled myself out of bed.

"Good morning," I said. Joel startled, since it wasn't normal for me to greet him in the morning.

"What are you doing up?" he asked.

"I have to ask you about this." I held up the small bottle of sniffing glue I had left on the dining room table. "Why do you have this?"

He paused, then like a teen caught with a pack of cigarettes, he protested that it wasn't his and belonged to one of his friends who had stayed at our place. I decided, at that moment, to not tell him what I saw in his bankbook. Instead, I told a lie of my own.

"So, umm, Josh called me last night at work to tell me something," I started. Josh was a gay friend of mine. "He called to say he was sorry about our marriage not working out. He says he saw you at The Barracks last week. I had to look up what The Barracks are. What the fuck, Joel?"

Joel's face went red, from the temples to his freshly shaved chin. I knew he was caught. I knew he had been doing things there he couldn't tell me about. His sexual orientation was crystal clear. I had ignored the evidence staring me in the face for years — the lack of sex, the male friends staying over, his attempts to make me feel inadequate. He told me he was just curious, would never go back to The Barracks and wanted to start a family with me. I really just needed to process what was happening so I end the conversation.

When I looked in his bankbook a week later and saw more recent charges from the same club, I paced the apartment, not knowing what to do. I called a friend at 1 a.m. and tried to get some guidance from her, but I had woken her and she really did not know what to say. I tried to go to sleep in the second bedroom, and when my tears turned into rage, I walked into our master bedroom, stood at his side of the bed and looked down at him with disgust. I was pissed off that he lied, that he potentially had sex with some stranger and then brought who knows what diseases into our hypothetical sex life. I was hurt that he was leading a double life and disappointed with myself for ignoring the signs that he was gay and allowing myself to be his beard. There was no longer any trust in our marriage.

I scared the shit out of him when I leaned down and hissed, "Wake up."

"What's wrong?" he asked.

"You're a liar. And stupid. You told me you weren't going back to that place and you went back the day after you promised you were done. Pack a bag and get the fuck out, we're done here."

"Calm down. We'll talk about this tomorrow night. I need to be at work in the morning."

"I don't care. Pack some clothes and go. Now." My voice got louder, and I felt my rage building. I think he saw it too.

"Where am I supposed to go at two in the morning? Can't we just talk about it?"

"Go to your mother's house. Your brother's. I don't care. You need to go now. This marriage is over. Get the fuck out." I felt angry, but I also felt really good. Relieved. Stronger than I had felt in years.

Ready to take on the single life and find a good man.

He moved all his clothing out two days later. He took some CDs. We talked rationally about what dishes, small appliances and knick-knacks he could take. A few things he took out of spite, and I didn't fight him about any of it. I learned to let go of the things I loved a long time ago when my mother tossed my Pound Puppy off the balcony. He packed everything he took from our marriage into 11 boxes, storing it all in his brother's basement. I never shed another tear for him after he moved out. My crying was all done during our marriage.

SUSHI & OTHER ENTREES

Dana Goldstein

23 JDATE

The day after Joel left, I woke up with new resolve. Despite having kicked my husband out, I felt comfortably alone and ready to move forward with my new life. The marriage had been over since our honeymoon, and I felt relieved to have finally admitted that and done something about it. I walked into our spare bedroom, and removed my ancient **IBM PC300** from my desk, making space for the new computer I had decided to buy. I needed to get onto this online dating platform I kept hearing about. I wasn't feeling any regret about my marriage dissolving. Not a shred of sadness in my heart. I called both of my parents and told them the news. My mother couldn't believe that I was OK; my father was genuinely sorry. "I'm not," I told him. "It's been over for a while."

Within hours of waking up, I had a new computer on my desk, running smoothly and I was trying to connect to the internet. Once my connection was live, I headed to JDate, the online dating service for Jewish people. It was new territory for me, and while it felt weird, it also felt safe. I could browse profiles, look at pictures and make decisions without having to risk my feelings. I had gained back almost 30 pounds over the two years of my marriage, and it stirred up all my feelings of inadequacy. It was an interesting contrast: feeling the pressure of unhappiness lift and the old familiar weight of insecurity settle in. Online dating was the perfect way to ease myself back into the dating scene.

A few of my single Jewish friends had tried online dating, and I'd heard not very positive things. They told me "Be prepared for a lot of weirdos," and "Don't believe everything you read," and "Guess what? Not every guy looks like his profile picture." So I was nervous, but excited at the same time to see what — or who — was out there. I worked on my free profile, answering the questions as clearly as I could. I was honest about everything, carefully skirting the stuff I didn't think strangers needed to know. There was a measure of safety in online dating, especially if you'd been out of the game for a long time. Having spent so many years unhappy, I knew without a doubt what I wanted and needed to be happy. I needed someone respectful, someone who made me cry only tears of laughter, who was encouraging and supportive, and who had nothing to hide. Online dating allowed me check people out while in my pajamas. I didn't have to do my hair or stress about what to wear until I was damned good and ready. When I got to the area where I needed to upload a photo, I realized I didn't have a single digital photo. I skipped that part for the time being and hit *Submit*. I was now part of the Jewish online dating scene.

I made the most of my day off and found a place that could scan a photo into a digital file. It was 2003, and affordable digital cameras were not yet commonplace. Getting photos digitized was expensive — in this case, I discovered it would cost me $30 to have one photo scanned to CD. I had to make sure I chose the best photo, since I was not going to pay to repeat this process. Ironically, the photo I selected was from my honeymoon: a colourful and fun photo of me in a moment of pure happiness, sailing in the Caribbean. I felt guilty about using that photo for a dating website, but I loved that my smile reached right up to my eyes.

I got home around 11 p.m. and immediately started up my computer tower and turned on my screen. While my computer started, I made myself a cup of coffee and poked around in my cupboard for a snack. There was really nothing in my cupboards other than some rice cakes, but I wouldn't eat them near my brand-new computer and get crumbs in the keyboard. So it was just me, my coffee and my CD in front of the glowing screen. When my computer was ready, I opened up my browser, navigated to JDate and logged in to discover I already had some messages in my profile inbox. It was so exciting to have this kind of interest already. One message was from the JDate people welcoming me to the service and telling me how much more access I could get with the paid service. There were two more messages from men on the site, asking for a photo. I checked out their profiles and sent messages back to both, telling them that my photo would soon be added.

I put the CD into the drive, clicked through to my profile, searched for the area where I could add my photo and clicked *Upload photo*. I navigated my way to the CD, clicked twice on the only file on the disc, and waited. It took a few minutes for the photo to upload and I was anxious. I'd not yet seen the quality of the file. Slowly, from the top, line-by-line, my image populated the photo space. It was a bit grainy, but it was good enough. I poked around the site looking at profiles until 1 a.m. I was not ready to start conversations with anyone yet, nor did I feel comfortable setting up dates. That felt too bold, too unfamiliar. I wasn't quite ready to take any risk right out of the gate. I wanted to wait and see if anyone reached out, or if the two men who had messaged me already would respond. It felt icky and dishonest to be talking to two men simultaneously. *I should probably wait and see what they are like before I look at anyone else*, I thought.

Within a few days, I was having an online conversation with one of the two men who initially messaged me. It was light chat: work, dating life, travel, favourite music/food/movies. He told me he was a movie fanatic, but when he said he'd never even heard of *Lawrence of Arabia*, I was stunned. It was a small thing but it really bothered me that someone who said he loved movies had never heard of this epic saga film. Having already been in a shitty relationship, I had set my bar high. No compromises. I was not going to set myself up for another relationship where I let a man tell me what I was worth. I wasn't going to repeat the complacent, co-operative behavior that had landed me in an unhappy marriage. I was going to silence my mother's voice telling me I was going to end up miserable and alone. If the online chat and emails didn't feel right, I decided, I didn't need to go any further. Trusting my gut, I just stopped responding to emails that made me feel out of sorts, or were salacious from the start, or were so full of spelling mistakes that I knew I was dealing with an idiot. I spent most of my non-working hours over the next week looking at profiles and really reading what was written.

A few days into my experience with JDate, I came across a profile that made me pay attention. Nice-looking man. Professed to love movies. Profession wasn't overinflated like some other profiles. I can't explain why, but in my gut, I felt like this man was telling it exactly like it was. No bullshit, just a simple statement of facts: this is who I am, what I do, what I like, how I spend my spare time, what I want in a relationship. I've got nothing to lose, I thought. I could have some online conversations, feel him out, see if my instincts were on the mark for once. I decided I would send this man a canned message — I wasn't yet ready to put all my cards on the table — and start the conversation.

"I really like your profile. What do you think of mine?"

He responded the same day. Polite and courteous. "Hi Dana,

it's nice to meet you." He asked some questions about where I grew up, what I did for work, how long I'd been on JDate. I had nothing to hide, so I was candid. Through a series of emails, we shared who we were and what we were. I told him I was married and now separated with a divorce pending. I told him I was working in retail, but I had a background in journalism and film. Yes, I liked *Star Trek* (but I really meant to say I liked *Star Wars*). Within a week, I nervously asked if he wanted to talk on the phone. This was the natural progression of online dating at the time.

We moved off email and had conversations on the phone that lasted into the wee hours of the night. I noticed three things over the course of those calls: he was highly intelligent, he made me laugh and I felt comfortable enough with him to tell him he was full of shit. All of that before I even met him in person.

After six hours of phone calls over four days, Jeff finally asked me out. It took a month for us to actually get on that date, since Jeff had a hectic travel schedule. We went for dinner at my favourite sushi restaurant where, I warned Jeff, the service was bad, but the food was delicious. We laughed at my embarrassment when it was pointed out that I needed to push a call button to summon a server to the room, a detail I hadn't known in all the three years I'd been coming there.

A month later, we were pregnant and living together, spending Christmas Day on the couch, binge watching *Buffy the Vampire Slayer* DVDs, eating steamed mussels and nibbling chips. We got engaged two months after that and married four months later with a small service and dinner in a private room at Moxie's. Eleven months after I sent that canned message, we welcomed our first child, Mason.

24 LEAVING

Aside from summers living abroad, I had never lived anywhere other than Toronto. I dreamed about working overseas, or moving to another part of Canada, but I never found the right opportunity. I was always looking for the chance to get away from everything I'd known and start fresh somewhere else, but my mother's voice invaded my brain and put fear into me about not being able to manage on my own. But when Jeff was offered the opportunity to move to Calgary, I emphatically said "Let's go".

When we first landed in Calgary for our house-hunting trip, with one baby in his carrier and the other being carried inside my belly, I was underwhelmed. It was March, and everything was so brown. As we drove our rental car through the industrial area around the airport, my first thought about Calgary was, *I'm not sure I can live here.* I did not share that thought with Jeff.

We checked into our hotel near the airport, fed Mason and picked up some basic groceries to fill the fridge for the week. We contacted our realtor and made a plan for where to meet the next day. For three days, we looked at houses in the southeast quadrant of Calgary. When our realtor was done with us for the day, we would drive around the city, trying to get a sense of what life might be like. I was on an emotional roller coaster: excited about buying our first house, terrified of what life might look like without being surrounded by people I knew, having fun looking at homes online, being sorely disappointed by what we could afford, feeling a great sense of adventure, realizing I would be raising my kids without any support from family.

When we finally found the perfect home for us — a 1,500-square-foot bungalow on a cul-de-sac — I had visions of domesticity. Jeff would be working from home, and I saw us all having breakfast together before I kissed Jeff goodbye as he headed down to his basement office, then Mason and I would venture out to the zoo, or the science centre or the playground. We moved into our home on a holiday weekend, Jeff building our new barbecue while Mason — who was a month away from taking his first steps — sat on the floor in the kitchen, playing with food storage containers and watching me organize things. For the first week, our lives were exactly as I imagined. We spent our time getting to know our home — where the furniture felt right, where the dishes should go, where we needed to display our treasures. We shopped for furniture, checked out the grocery stores, cooked dinner together in our bright, white kitchen.

We'd been living in our new home for a couple of weeks when Jeff left for a business trip. He woke me to kiss me and say goodbye. I laid in bed, unable to fall back asleep, feeling loneliness creep over me. I shook it off, made myself a coffee and settled in at my computer to find something fun for Mason and I to do for the weekend. I learned about the Lilac Festival, a one-day pedestrian event along Fourth Street in downtown Calgary. The idea of being outside, pushing Mason in the stroller while listening to music and shopping the artistic vendors, was appealing to me. I entered a random address on Fourth Street into my new GPS unit and let it navigate me in the right direction. I found parking on a side street and followed the small groups of people walking down the street, assuming they were heading to the festival. As we neared Fourth Street, I could hear music playing, and the buzz of voices that comes from a large crowd. I passed the bright orange barriers blocking vehicle access to the street and stopped, assessing the crowds. I looked down at Mason, who was comfortable in his stroller and looking around at all the activity.

"Ready, buddy?" I asked.

"Go, Mama," he answered, pointing his chubby nine-month-old finger to the crowd.

We wandered the street for the next two hours. We stopped to listen to music, eat some food and look at the booths. The farther down the street we went, the sadder and lonelier I felt. I missed my husband. I watched families move together through the festival; I noticed clusters of friends laughing and sharing the experience.

Sadness and loneliness hit me like a shit-ton of bricks. It's a pattern: every time someone leaves me, my need to feed is triggered. I will eat whatever junk food I can get my hands on, and I will eat until I am sick to my stomach. I fill the void, consuming my subconscious fear with every single bite. I know that whoever left (usually my husband) will be coming back, and I should know better by now, but something deep within takes over when I am alone. I can feel the anxiety creeping up on me, days before departure, but I don't try to divert my feeding frenzy.

Fear not only triggers eating binges; it drives complacency. I accept things that should never be acceptable: the berating from my in-the-closet first husband, the invasion into my psyche of the outside voices that tell me I am not good enough, the peripheral treatment from the people who are supposed to be my friends. We all make foolish choices and allow ourselves to get hurt. But one day, you will snap. You will decide that you have had enough. You will find your inner strength, you will have the guts to go it alone. When you finally decide that it's time to move forward, life will suck for 15 minutes, and then you'll realize that you are so much better off.

I have carried the burden of betrayal into every period of my life. I take it personally — deeply and painfully — when the people I let into my life stab me in the back. My husband says I invite the betrayal in because I expect it to happen with every friend I make. After more than a decade of marriage, my husband can recognize the signs — the anxiety, the tense shoulders, the challenging and defensive stance I take during conversations.

"I'm not your parents or your first husband," he reminds me when I am heading toward the cliff of mistrust. Every time he says it, I can feel myself being reeled in from the edge. I can trust him. He has proven that over and over again. Maybe I subconsciously look for the betrayal and because of that, I manifest it in my social groups. I try to fit in, to be a giving, trusting and caring friend, but a part of me is holding back. I let my safety screen roll down only partway, because without fail, I will need to roll it back up when the hurt happens.

I felt pain in my heart and a lump in my chest and it dawned on me that Mason and I were all we had that day at the festival. Jeff would be travelling on a regular basis, and if I didn't find some friends, I would wither. I am a social person. I need to interact with others. When Mason and I got home from the festival and he went down for a nap, I headed to my computer, looking for a local social network for moms.

25 COOKIES

I need people, either in real life or online. In Toronto, I had found an online bulletin board for local moms and it made being a first-time mom so much easier. We shared our successes and failures, our joys and frustrations. I chatted with moms who had a child the same age as Mason. We met for coffee one afternoon and that meeting stuck. We are still friends to this day. So it seemed logical to me to try to find a similar online group based in my new city. I stumbled upon Calgary Moms, a community forum for candid conversation and bitch sessions, where anyone could ask any kind of question and get real and relevant answers. Within months of joining the site, I was checking the forums several times per day and engaging in conversations. "C-moms," as all of us on the site called it, slowly became my village.

It wasn't until after Westin was born that I moved into meeting these people for real. There were some moms' night-out gatherings, and Halloween and Christmas parties, but I was too pregnant for some and breastfeeding a newborn during some of the others. Jeff was still travelling a great deal, and I wasn't ready to leave my children with a babysitter. In the first two years on the site, I became a moderator, went on weekend escapes in the Rocky Mountains with around 20 of the moms, and I had a place to feel like a member of a community.

When my boys were between the ages of two and three, I hosted a play date in our house every Monday morning. The Monday Blues, as it came to be known, was a social and emotional lifesaver for me. The Monday Blues was a way for stay-at-home moms to launch the week on a positive note. Husbands were back to work, weekend events were over, and once again, we were faced with the solitude that comes with making the choice to stay home and raise our children. I had taken over the weekly gathering from another mom who had moved back to Ontario, and I cherished those mornings for the friendships (including some that have lasted more than a decade, and across a country), the laughter and the musical noise of little children in every corner of my home. These play dates gave me a reason to clean my house on Monday afternoons, but mostly, I was just happy to not feel so alone, to have other moms to talk to who were trying to get through the mundane duties of staying at home. All the kids in Monday Blues were under four, and my house was left a mess of drool, food bits, misplaced toys and boogers. Don't get me wrong, I was grateful for the opportunity to stay home, raise our kids and host my friends. Most days, anyway. Some days, I wanted to chuck it all away, play Bejeweled and let the kids fend for themselves.

The night before Monday Blues was usually a late one for me. Once the boys went to bed, I would stay up, baking cookies for the group. On any given Monday, there could be as many as 30 people — big and little — in my house and they needed to be fed. Late-night baking was not a chore; I had such joy in my heart for the people I met online and who had become my support system in real life. Baking cookies for this group was healthy for me.

I never considered myself a cook or a baker. In the '70s, with a single working mom, our life was all about prepared foods and convenience. Vegetables came in a can, pasta came in a box with powdered cheese sauce, breakfast pastry was wrapped in thick paper packaging that when ripped open released the smell of sugary sweetness. By the age of 10, I knew how to boil veggies, broil a steak in the oven, make Kraft Dinner and the perfect toasting time for Pop Tarts. Baking was never done in my house. Once in a blue moon, we would have a roll of Pillsbury cookies.

When I met Jeff, I would joke about how he needed to have low expectations of what I could do in the kitchen. He could care less, and happily devoured everything I ever made for us, even the stuff he hated. We were in the early stages of our relationship, the part where all the shitty things are paled by the great sex. We could have consumed burned soup and been delighted. In a strange twist, my husband became keenly interested in cooking about 12 years into our marriage, and is now rocking the meals. He is a way better cook than I am. Now, he has the benefit of YouTube to teach him, and fortunately, there is no shortage of beautiful women with channels who want to teach him. In this family, he has become the cook, but I have become the baker. I love the process and I love the chemistry, but more than anything, I love the results.

On the morning of Monday Blues, as I waited for my friends to arrive, I would look around my kitchen, eyeing the plate of oatmeal chocolate chip cookies I baked, and it would click why I was so tired. Sugar fatigue. I think what made me tired is the unreasonable number of cookies I devoured the night before.

See, this is how it would go. I would bake five dozen cookies. After decades of being a sub-par cook and baker, I had doubts about their taste, so I would sample them. Still not convinced, I would enlist the help of my husband. He'd say they're delicious, but, not prone to trusting people at their word, I wouldn't believe him. So, I would try another. When I determined that they *were* good, I would start packing them away in containers. About two-thirds of the way through, I would realize the container I chose wasn't large enough to accommodate five dozen (minus the samples) cookies. I would keep trying with different containers, all to no avail.

This was a ritual that repeated itself, week after week. Let's call it the "Pretend I'm surprised when I really know better and I've been through this a million times" dance.

Step 1 Bake cookies as small as possible. Smaller cookies means you can trick your brain into believing that eating 15 small cookies is nowhere near as bad as eating four regular-size ones.

Step 2 Immediately and repeatedly test cookies until you are certain they are tasty. After cookies have cooled completely, perform another taste test with your evening cup of tea.

Step 3 Attempt to store cookies in containers that can only hold 4.5 dozen cookies. Store remaining cookies in your stomach.

Step 4 The next day, prepare cookies on a serving plate. Check for freshness by eating a few more.

Step 5 Serve cookies. Allow your guests to indulge themselves first, then eat some yourself to reassure your guests that you are not trying to poison them.

Step 6 Send some cookies away with your guests. Give most of them away, but hang on to some. After all, they were darn good cookies.

Dana Goldstein

26 YOGA

I am not a yoga fan. I know there are people who absolutely love yoga, and I am fully aware of the benefits, but there are some things about yoga that people don't tell you — just like there are some ugly bits about pregnancy and childbirth that you only find out about through experience.

I once decided to try a beginner class requiring extremely basic skills. The class focused on breathing and stretching the muscles, so I wasn't expected to put my ankle behind my head in this session. Good thing, because there is little chance I could get my thigh over my head without knocking myself out. We started with breathing into the stomach. No problem. Then we worked on breathing into the sternum and the chest. I hadn't seen my ribs in four years and after two kids my chest had sort of worked itself downward into that region. I thought I was breathing into the sternum, but then I felt my boobs hit my chin, and things became confused.

The legs and butt were next. Various stretches and bends and twists. I am pretty flexible, so that wasn't an issue. What happened was my thighs got in the way. It may not have looked like it, but my butt *was* on the floor and my legs *were* up in the air. It was just tough to tell where they separated. But believe me, my lower back knew the difference, because it was starting to hurt. I messed things up by shifting my weight. My legs, so used to taking the brunt of my bulk, were now laughing their ... well ... ass off, because they were happily in the air enjoying a break while my back was groaning. And I completely lost all focus on my breathing. Why? Because as I brought my legs to my chest, I was focused on one other thing: trying not to pass gas. Still, I kept trying the stretches, while trying not to let one go.

I looked around at my friends, to see if they were suffering the same way, and yes, they absolutely were. Then it happened. Someone in the class let one go. For the next 30 minutes, my friends and I tried desperately not to look at each other, because when we did, we released into uncontrollable giggles. When the instructor started grunting and moaning like she was in a porn movie, I had to leave the room and let the hysterics take over. I lost control of my breathing while trying not to lose control of my bladder. When I settled down enough to think I could manage to finish the class, one of my friends emerged. One glance and we were both holding our sides, wiping our tears and had to move into the hallway far from the class so we didn't disturb the fire-breathing meditation happening. It was ridiculous.

Yeah, yoga is not for me.

27 BEST DIET EVER

The last time I lost a significant amount of weight was when I was extremely ill in 2015. I felt the worst I have ever felt in my whole life, including having pushed out two babies, having late-diagnosed pneumonia and a case of shingles. I emerged from diverticulitis, an infection in the pouches of my digestive track, with a plan to eliminate red meat from my diet and the best results a fat girl could ask for: 15 pounds lighter. Getting violently ill enough to lose a ton of weight is a secret wish of anyone who has a lot of weight to lose. Anyone who denies this is lying. This sentiment was perfectly captured in a waste of a movie in the late '90s, when one of the characters in *Romy and Michelle's High School Reunion* declared mono to be "the best diet ever." Idiotic movie, brilliant observation. In more recent cinematic history, in *The Devil Wears Prada,* one of the characters observes she is "one stomach flu away from my goal weight."

I had long wished for a quick start to weight loss, but diverticulitis is not something I want to repeat. I was in bed for two weeks, unable to eat, but it took another week before I even had the strength to make a cup of tea. I cried from frustration when all my energy was sapped from the effort it took to go to the bathroom. The antibiotics were burning in my empty stomach, but I could not even ingest a cracker without feeling like I was going to throw up. The mere act of chewing was a struggle. I slept for 10-plus hours at night and napped my way through the day.

I did not miss food at all when I was ill. That was a first for me. I'd been sick before, but after a day or two, the usual cravings returned. I've been able to eat normally through every illness I have ever had, except for food poisoning and diverticulitis. The really stupid thing is that instead of taking the weight loss and using it as a launching point for a major change, I returned to the old habits and put on 35 pounds over the following year and a half. Stupid waste of an effortless weight loss. I told myself the junk is OK because I had just lost a bunch of weight, my body was still not used to eating, everything will just pass through my system, it's only a few chips/cookies/M&Ms. I snacked myself back to the weight I was before my illness and packed on even more weight, one bite, lick and taste at a time.

I should know better when it comes to weight-related illnesses. My father recently lost his right leg above the knee, the result of complications from diabetes, and he is currently in a home, 3,000 kilometres away from where I live. I am tortured by feeling compassion, pity, apathy and rage. My body is suffering — I vacillate between wanting to eat everything in sight and eating nothing at all; my emotions are manifesting themselves as pain in my shoulders, headaches (which are a rarity for me) and extreme fatigue.

My husband and I offered to make space for my dad in whatever home we were living in, wherever we were living. We offered to move to a house that had an in-law apartment and he could come and go as he pleased. When he was forced to sell his house to cover the debts he accumulated over 50 years of gambling, we made the same offers again. I told him to come spend his golden years with his only child and grandsons. He declined, opting to live in the minivan we gave him. He blew through the $400,000 he yielded from the house sale in three years, gambling away everything he had, rather than move to be close to family, living a nice life in a condo.

Now, living in a government-subsidized home that is not wheelchair accessible, with no one to coddle him, he is realizing how badly he governed himself. At 74, he is alone and broke, but not at all repentant. He has lost his right leg to diabetes, losing his ability to drive and his freedom. He's asked if we have space for him in our house and, with a great deal of difficulty, I have repeatedly said no. That ship has sailed. I cannot ask my husband and children to watch me become my father's caregiver and see the resentment stewing inside me. I owe him nothing. He was never there for me, not emotionally, not financially.

It hurts me to have to turn my back on him. For all the hurt I endured, he is still my father. And that is the father wound, the pain of the little girl who just wanted her dad. A young woman who watched normal father-daughter relationships from the sidelines and wished she had the same kind of life.

28 MUSINGS ABOUT MENOPAUSE

When you have a lot of weight to lose, it seems like the end will never come. You diet and you exercise and you deprive yourself and at the end of the week, the scale has barely moved.

It's exhausting.

Now, I realize that people lose weight in different ways, but it has never seemed fair to me the way I lose weight. For some people, 10 pounds is very noticeable. For others, you can only notice it from the way they hold their heads a bit higher. On my frame, a 10-pound loss is only obvious to me. I don't have to step on the scale to know I've lost weight. I just step in to my shoes, because that's where I lose it first. After my feet have shrunk a size, the weight loss will move on to my face. I lose my chins and then my chubby cheeks, and people look at me weird. They know something is different, but can't quite figure it out. I'll help you out — it's that my head now looks too small for my body. As I lose more weight, the changes become more evident from the neck down. After the face, it's the boobs — first the ones in front, then the back boobs. Then it's a natural progression: waist, hips, butt. But it takes forever for the weight loss to show on my derrière. Let's not even talk about the thighs. And now that I'm past 40 and closer to 50, losing weight is even harder. If I could tell my 20-year-old self one thing, it would be to commit to a fitness regime and stop counting on tomorrow to go on a diet.

Menopause has wreaked havoc on my body. For the last six years, I have been a helpless host for all the crap going on with my ovaries. Periods that come as they please are bad enough, but I have struggled with cravings that last for weeks. And then, when the cravings stop, no period, but my gut has expanded and it's harder to move. I feel like I want to rebel against this new body, but I am too freaking tired. My feet swell for no reason. My body sometimes aches when I get out of bed. The combination of age and body weight leaves me breathless at the top of the stairs. One of my ankles is weak and every now and then will twist slightly the wrong way and send pain throughout my leg.

Some days, my need for junk food is so bad that I behave like a newly licensed driver, finding any excuse to get behind the wheel.

"We need toothpaste," my husband says.

"I'll go to the drugstore after dinner," I'll say.

"We don't need it right now, we just need to add it to our list for our next drugstore run."

I am hugely disappointed. When I crave garbage food, tasks that would normally be a pain in the ass suddenly become all-important and no trouble at all. Just so I can feed my need. Sometimes, when I am sitting in my car, eating my chips, I think my licence and my money should just be taken away from me. I should not be allowed to go anywhere near a store that sells junk food ever again. That would leave me with trips to the pet supply store.

I think about diabetes, since both my parents have Type 2. People say, "Listen to your body," but that is hard when my body is so indecisive about what it wants, like a picky eater at a buffet. I can't seem to get a handle on what my body wants from me. For fuck's sake, I am trying. To give you some idea of what my body is saying to me, let's listen in to a conversation:

Morning!

I don't want to wake up.

Get up. You have to pee.

It's warm under the blankets. I can hold it.

You've been holding it since 3:30 a.m. Why do you think you can't fall back asleep?

Because I've got too much on my mind.

Stop thinking about work. There is nothing that needs to be done at 4:15 am.

But the alarm is going to go off in 45 minutes. I want some more sleep. Shush please.

That's a weird popping from my hip.

Do you think I am finally breaking under all the weight?

Today will be a juicing day. I need to cleanse the cookies I ate yesterday. I'll get on the bike too.

Alarm goes off.

Shit.

OK, here we go. One leg out. Good. No pain. Second leg out. Still no pain. Shoulders are a little tight.

Coffeecoffeecoffeecoffeecoffeecoffeecoffeecoffeecoffeecoffeecoffee.

Then I waddle down the stairs, hanging onto the banisters, going sideways, one step at a time, to ease the stress on the knees.

Before I have even had breakfast, I have already had several nonsensical conversations in my head. I like to think I am dialed into what my body is talking about, but it's more confusing than trying to decipher an 18-month-old's babble. All I know for sure is that I have lost control. Fifteen years ago, working out every day would have yielded a weekly five-pound weight loss. That is not the case anymore. These days, working out every day usually results in an injury or extreme fatigue or even worse, hopeless frustration. That's what I'm faced with on a daily basis. The knowledge of what my body once could do and the realization of my new limitations is heartbreaking. When I stick with a regime for months, there is no guarantee of weight loss. There is in fact a high probability of weight gain. I find myself Googling "How to lose 100 pounds without exercise" or "How to flip your metabolism after menopause" and find only bad news: Can't be done. Do not pass Go.

29 HUMILIATION

There are different degrees of public humiliation, and some are worse than others.

The humiliation from slipping on the ice or tripping over your own feet is commonplace and we have all experienced that moment of "I hope nobody saw that."

The humiliation from walking around with toilet paper trailing from the bottom of your shoe.

The humiliation of a clingy sock being stuck to your butt.

The humiliation from realizing you don't have enough cash to pay for your groceries, and your credit card is declined.

The humiliation of falling into a bucket of ferret poop and not being able to tie your jacket around your waist to cover your wet ass.

These are all instances of passive humiliation. The universe is simply working against you. Peel off the toilet paper and move on. But then there are examples of deliberate humiliation.

Mean kids at school who make mooing noises when you walk by.

Teenagers who grab onto the lockers, yelling "Earthquake!" as you move down the hallway.

Strangers who puff their cheeks out at you as you pull up next to them at a stop light.

People who have the nerve to take something out of your shopping cart and act like they are doing you a favour.

I suffered the greatest humiliations from my mother, who had no qualms about hollering to me from the other side of a store, "Dana, the bras are over here!" or "Dana, I found the pants you like in a size 18!" My mother isn't oblivious to how embarrassing she can be; she deliberately discounts my feelings, just as she minimizes my accomplishments.

"Why the fuck can you not remember what it is I do?"

I said this after I'd already slammed the phone down, frustrated by yet another conversation with my mother. It's been like this my whole life: she calls, asks me some perfunctory questions about my life, my work, my kids, my husband (but only when she is not mad at him and needs to gossip) and then she moves on to tell me about the wonderful lives her friends' kids have. How successful they are. How they ask their mothers to travel with them.

Because they have mothers they actually like, I think.

Today, for the 30th time, she asked me how the insurance business is going. I paused, wondering for the 30th time if this was a classic symptom of age-related dementia, but I dismissed that. It was a classic symptom of my mother who can't retain the fact that I haven't liked purple onions since I could chew my own food, let alone the fact that I don't work in the insurance business. I am a legal videographer, sent by lawyers working on accident insurance cases to record the medical appointments of plaintiffs. I record legal depositions, sometimes in very high-profile cases that people are talking about and that she has read about in the newspaper. It's not complicated to remember what it is I do.

I've always been jealous of the parent-child relationships I see around me. Parents who are present and supportive. Parents who drop everything when a child is in need. It wasn't until I was in my mid-30s, married to Jeff with two kids of my own, that I began to understand the nature of my parents.

My mother has never played a game of chess, but she managed to checkmate my life until I realized I didn't have to play the game her way. Her moves are calculated, her words evasive, but she backs me into a corner every time. I have spent my life apologizing for things that needed no apology: *I'm sorry I went out with my friends* (when you wanted me home to make sure I recorded *Dynasty* on the VCR). *I'm sorry I bought you the wrong dishes for Mother's Day* (after I took public transit to the store, switching busses twice, carrying an awkward and heavy box). *I'm sorry I was mean to you* (after you killed my high school social life). She has revised history to serve her needs, and has denied saying hateful, hurtful things to me, like what she said at the dance recital. That comment has stuck with me and every time she casually tosses a snide comment in my direction, my defenses go up. My mother stopped talking to me during my first pregnancy because I was moody and yelled at her. My husband can vouch for this one. We didn't speak until I called to tell her I was in labour.

"Are you calling to tell me, or are you calling because you want me there?" I paused for a second, contemplating how to answer. No, I didn't want her there, but this was her first grandchild and I felt a duty to her.

She came to the hospital, and while I was floating in epidural bliss, she proceeded to explain to Jeff how much I owed her for what she gave up for me. She denied this conversation later, just as she changed the fact that she stopped speaking to me, to shift the blame my way. She has no qualms about leaving spiteful messages on voicemail, and I have played some of these for my husband to prove to him that I am not making it up.

Hi Dana. I just wanted to let you know that I no longer have a daughter. Have a nice life.

Hi Dana, I hope you are happy with your new family, since you find so much wrong with the one you already have.

Hello. In case you were curious, I got rid of all the things you left in my house. Goodbye.

Her tone is always a combination of condescending and sarcastic. It's a tone I have been listening to my whole life. It signals that my mother is trying to control the situation and punish me for something I may or may not have done. There is nothing nurturing or sensitive about her. For years, I craved the kind of loving relationship I saw my friends had with their mothers. I did everything I could to please her, to make her love me and want to spend time with me. I absorbed her emotional problems as my own, trying to heal them and show her I was worthy of her love. I let her control everything in my life, including my relationship with my father.

I'm done now. I've grown up. I've put my big-girl panties on. She no longer gets to decide where the conversation goes and when the conversation ends. My life happens in my voice now.

30 THE GAME OF LIFE

Not too long ago, we took our boys to get fitted for their first real suits. Just typing that sentence brings tears to my eyes. They are in the tween years now, no longer little boys and well on their way to becoming young men. As they stood in front of the triple mirrors in full dress — jacket, shirt, tie, pants and dress shoes — I had a hard time accepting how fast time is passing. My babies were growing up while I slept, while I worked and while I wasn't looking. But damn, they looked good in suits.

Mason, my 12-year-old, has no problem with confidence. He sometimes borders on egomaniacal but that is not the result of us constantly telling him how amazing he is. Of course, we boost his confidence, and he has grown comfortable with the fact that he is usually the shortest kid in his class. His sense of self is remarkable given that we yanked him away from his friends so often; he's attended six schools since nursery school. Westin, my 11-year-old, is just starting to settle into his personality. He is a prankster, and it took a great deal of focus for him to not deliberately trip off the podium at the suit shop and fake a fall into the mirrors. He is extremely comfortable being alone, which is a blessing and a curse; people sometimes assume he is uninterested in socializing but he's just lost in his own world.

I look at these boys with awe. So secure, so sure, so healthy. How I managed to shirk the toxicity of my mother and not pass that on to my kids or bring it into my marriage is beyond me. I can't say I consciously made that happen with my husband and our two amazing sons, but I somehow ended up with a man who understood my origins and two boys who are smart, sensitive and funny.

As the boys were having their pants pinned for tailoring and I was taking photos, I caught sight of myself in the mirror. In three seconds, my mood went from one of awe to one of shame. I can't believe just how large I have gotten. I'm sure I have body dysmorphic disorder: the condition where you think your body looks one way when in fact it looks another. I think I am smaller than I truly am. Looking at myself in the mirror at home, when I am standing, sucking in the gut a bit, adjusting my clothes to hide the rolls, is very different from catching a glimpse of my girth when I am sitting down, relaxed and not trying to hide anything. I realized in that three-second blip that this is exactly how other people see me. I was thoroughly disgusted with myself.

I wondered how soon I could slip away from my family and find a bag of chips. Where in the next few hours before I go to bed could I find a reason to sneak away on my own? Maybe we could stop for snacks on our way home. It was family game night, after all. We needed treats.

As an only child, I always wanted to play board games. My mother, a single working mom, was either too tired or completely uninterested. I just wanted to play, to laugh like the kids I saw in the TV commercials who played Operation. Then, when I had my own two kids 14 months apart, I found myself too tired or completely uninterested. With my husband away for work most of the time, I had little energy or desire to engage at the end of the day. Still stuck to the idea of playing as a family, I purchased Operation and Candy Land when the boys were old enough to play. Neither game took much focus, and these boys would happily play for an hour or more. Sometimes even without me.

Now, when our family game nights are running smoothly and we are all laughing, trying not to spit out our hot chocolate, we have enriching conversations. We talk about life issues veiled in the play on the board. Monopoly morphs into conversations about poverty, excess and money management. The Game of Life triggers talks about life choices, the cost of raising kids and the value of education. Risk becomes an exercise in patience, planning and anger management. We talk about things that matter to our pre-teen boys: friendships, plans for the summer, what's going on in their school lives. But we also find ourselves blurting out the things we struggle with, as if the gaming environment is a shield for our vulnerability. I can easily talk about my own childhood, Jeff will voice his frustrations about life, and our boys will open up and candidly share what's going on in their worlds. I wasn't expecting family game night to be a mini-therapy session. I had no inkling that one day, over a game of Risk, we would be talking about where we all need to go when we are in a dark, angry place. It was our 12-year-old who sparked that conversation, when he observed his father's frustration with the game.

"Dad, just chill. I don't want you to get mad and go hide in the basement and play Civilization. That's where you hide when you get angry."

I started laughing, not only because he was right, but because he was so observant.

"I look to my video games too when I need to cool down," he added.

"I look to Super Smash Bros. when I get angry," our 11-year-old jumped in.

"I look to the bottom of a bag of chips," I said.

We all laughed at my witty remark, but we all knew this was no joke. That is exactly where I go when I am emotionally stressed.

31 THE ROLLER COASTER

When you spend most of your life in the plus-size zone, you have more than one bottom. I'm not talking about the ridge formed by my ample ass, separating the upper gluteus from the lower portion. The bottom is where you hit an emotional low, when you face a humiliation so deeply painful, or when you have a realization that spurs you forward to make a change for the better. For some bad habits, you only need the one epiphany, like the one when I made the decision to quit smoking at the age of 42. That one hit me as I was standing outside a children's museum in Rochester, New York, in February, with no coat on and no shelter from the fat, wet snowflakes blowing in my face, while my shaking, frozen hands brought my cigarette to my lips.

It's different for weight loss, though. I've had so many incidents of shame and pain, and every one has spurred me toward a change for the better. But before I can do that, I need to drown my grief with junk food. I need to feel sorry for myself. Frustrated. Numb. Helpless. Alone. I consume my pain — always with salty snacks — and then I go to sleep, thinking about how that was my last bag of chips and tomorrow morning I am having fruit for breakfast. The humiliation from earlier in the day has settled into my fat cells, adding to my girth while it wears away my happiness.

Weight loss for me is a roller coaster ride, but one where I get stuck in the curve of an upside-down loop. I am terrified and helpless. My heart races, and I make a dozen promises to my god and my body. I wait for the uncertainty to end and I find acceptance for a while. But then there is an unexpected jerking motion and the fear comes roaring back.

I love amusement parks. I love the thrill of the roller coasters, the smells of deep-fried everything, the lights and the sounds. As soon as our kids were old enough we started visiting amusement parks, starting with Disneyland. There is such joy in watching my children discover their stomach flips on the roller coasters, seeing the wonder on their faces when they experience life-size animatronics and hearing their laughter even while standing in line.

When The Wizarding World of Harry Potter opened at Universal Orlando Resort, it was a torturous wait until the boys were old enough to read the Harry Potter series. Seven years passed between the opening of the first Harry Potter attraction and the day we stood in line under the shadow of Hogwarts. We kept our visit to Universal a secret from the boys, only revealing our plan once we were in Orlando, the night before we went to the park. The boys were excited, and over dinner, we talked animatedly about Harry, Ron and Hermione, Gringotts, Ollivanders and Diagon Alley.

After dinner, we headed to our hotel to check in for the first of our four-night stay. I am not a snob about hotel rooms, but this was the most disgusting one I had ever been in. My husband travels a great deal for business, and stays in a particular chain and continually earns us points for future free stays. When we travel as a family, we stay in those same chains and we always have a great experience. Except this time.

I always laugh at Jeff because he will not walk barefoot in a hotel room. He has travel slippers. I, on the other hand, will go barefoot at any opportunity. I am not bothered by what might be on the floor. But at this hotel, as soon as my bare feet hit the floor, I could feel the grime, like a waxy film on the carpet. As we were changing for dinner, Jeff looked over at me and started laughing. I was standing on my shoes. I went to sit on a chair, but diverted to the bathroom for a towel to place over the stains on the seat.

"After dinner, can we look at booking something else?" I asked.

Jeff was delighted and relieved. He did not want to spend the next four nights in this room either, but after 12 years of marriage, he knew that if he brought it up, I'd freak out about the early checkout charges and the inflated price we would have to pay for better accommodations. Not this time, I assured him. I would lose less sleep about the money than I would imagining what was climbing into our suitcases once the lights were out.

"Promise?" he said, not believing that I wouldn't be obsessing over the money for the rest of our trip.

I laughed. "I promise. I can't stay here."

After dinner, Jeff fired up his computer and we began looking for an alternative hotel. Ever the optimist, I was sure that we would find something acceptable. We were fortunate to find a room at Cabana Bay at Universal Studios for $50 per night more than we were paying for our current hotel. We booked it, excited about getting there the next day.

The next morning started with great enthusiasm.

Cabana Bay fulfilled its promise of being a wonderful place to stay. It was a throwback to the motels of the '50s and '60s. For Jeff and I, it was a reminder of our beloved childhood stays in Miami Beach: post-modern and brightly coloured furniture, a cafeteria-style restaurant, Formica everywhere, but no seniors sitting on the veranda. Most importantly, the room was spotless and comfortable. As a perk, it was a Universal property. That meant early access to Universal Studios, where The Wizarding World of Harry Potter is, a full hour before it opened to the public.

We were at the park for the advanced 8 a.m. opening. We followed the rush of people to the line for the Harry Potter and the Forbidden Journey ride, excitedly absorbing all the details of Hogwarts, chatting about Quidditch, mandrakes and the recent death of Alan Rickman, the actor who played Professor Snape in the films. My boys and I share an equally deep appreciation and love for Harry Potter. My husband, who has not read the books, was joyfully enjoying our enthusiasm.

When we finally got to the front of the line, my enthusiasm changed to horror in a heartbeat when we were pulled away from climbing into the ride car, and I was asked to try to fit into the sample seat they had off to the left of the line. I smiled and tried to carry on happily as I squished myself into the seat, silently praying for the harness to close. I shifted back as far as I could, trying to manipulate my rolls, willing them to be pliable enough. I tried not to think of the whole line of people who were watching this play out. All I could think was, *Please, please, please let me fit. Please don't make this a bad experience for my kids.*

But I didn't fit and I was denied entry to the ride. As we were escorted to the appropriately labelled cargo elevator, my face burned. I did my best not to burst into tears. The young attendant handed me a pass to get us to the front of the line for a different ride and I glanced at my husband only to see pity all over his face. I turned my body slightly away from my family, looking down and away as I cried.

My eldest broke the silence. "Wow, that must have been embarrassing," he said. I was mortified that he was being so glib and insensitive. In hindsight, I think he was trying to be empathetic, a skill that was still developing in my 12-year-old son.

I said nothing, completely unable to speak. When the doors of the elevator opened, I was surprised when we emerged in another part of the Forbidden Journey ride. Another attendant was waiting for us, to escort us to a ride car that was parked on siding tracks. I could see the animations in the ride from the siding, and I watched as full ride cars whizzed by into the depths of the ride. As we settled into our ride car seats, I was so grateful for the dividers that separated each of us, preventing my kids and husband from seeing me. I was in full-on tears. I was so uncomfortable in the ride car, the harness digging into my stomach. The attendant tried to have a light-hearted conversation with us, but I imagine that's not an easy role when you are working with the obese riders. I have no idea if the ride car was specially reinforced and stabilized, or if we missed part of the ride. All I could focus on was being straddled between unbelievable shame and trying to keep the excitement going for my kids.

Once we launched into the ride, I tried to forget what had just happened and let the magic of the ride take over, but my joy was sucked out of me. I was blank, emotionless and not the least bit interested in a trip I'd been looking forward to for ages.

When we emerged and I awkwardly removed myself from the

seat, I wiped my face and planted a smile on my face, faking my glee while trying to engage the energy of my kids. My husband looked so sad for me, it was heartbreaking. Having once been an obese person, he understood the humiliation, but he also knew how much I was looking forward to the ride. He was genuinely sad for me and enraged with the park for what had happened. The rest of our visit in the park was tarnished for me, and I found no pleasure in anything. The whole day disappeared into that dark, humiliating bottom. For the first time in my life, I had no interest in food. My grief consumed me, instead of me wanting to consume my grief.

32 MAKAPU'U LIGHTHOUSE POINT

We are a little family of part-time explorers, sometimes veering off the path to discover gorgeous places and spaces, but we aren't hard-core hikers who travel with our Salomon hiking boots. As I get older — and heavier — this is getting harder for me to do. The last few vacations, I have been really feeling my girth. I have become keenly aware that my body is slowly collapsing under its weight. This is not sitting well with me.

One of our great joys is hiking near the ocean when we are in Hawaii. The salty spray from the Pacific, the warm breezes carried by the tropical winds and the wildlife darting across our path give us our *ha* (the Hawaiian word for "breath of life"). We are never alone on these journeys, as most trails we take are popular with other hikers, amateur and professional.

Flipping through the guidebook we picked up at the car rental depot, looking for things to do in Oahu on a recent trip, I came across the pages dedicated to hiking. First, I read about Diamond Head, a 700-foot climb to the top of the famous crater that marks the Honolulu skyline. Everyone I know of who has done this hike has given me this advice: go early, take lots of water and be prepared to work hard. And this is from people who are somewhat fit and light. Nope, this hike is not for me, not now anyways.

The description for another hike, the Makapu'u Lighthouse Trail, sounded more like my kind of deal.

I read the paragraph out loud to my husband. "Let's try this one," I said. "It sounds lovely." He agreed and we added it to our itinerary.

"A two-mile, paved trail overlooking the lighthouse. This moderately easy hike pays off with breathtaking views of the indigo ocean and Oahu's eastern, or windward, coast. You can even see the island of Molokai in the distance. Two other smaller islands, Mānana (the larger of the two, also known as Rabbit Island) and Kaohikaipu are also visible just offshore."

The day of the hike broke perfectly, like every day we ever have in Hawaii. We were not in any great rush to get there, though. We had breakfast and packed lunches. We savoured our coffee out on the *lanai*, breathing in the ocean, watching the waves break. It was idyllic. On the 54-minute drive, traffic was normal on H-1, one of three major highways on Oahu. We hit a bit of backup just west of Honolulu, but nothing really agitated us. We were in Hawaii for crying out loud. In Hawaii, even the bad days are good days. We drove in a comfortable and happy silence. Once we were east of Honolulu and past Waikiki beach, we made our way onto Kalanianaole Highway. This is the part of the drive that I was grateful to not be the one driving, perfectly content with the opportunity to absorb the scenery. For the next 10 miles, all I could see was ocean and the lush green volcanic formations of the mountains. We passed heavy traffic lined up outside Hanauma Bay, a snorkeller's haven famous for its calm waters and spectacular sea life. I mentally added it to my list for our next trip.

As I watched the ocean, the brilliant blue waves smashing on the rocks, my mind drifted to last year, when we had booked a catamaran and snorkel excursion. My husband and youngest had a mild case of seasickness and stayed on the boat when we anchored to snorkel. My eldest gave it a good shot, but the newness of snorkeling coupled with the open ocean was a bit too intimidating for him. He tried though, getting into the water, snorkel tube in his mouth and mask on, but he wouldn't even dip his face into the water. After 15 minutes of me trying to encourage him to just peek under the surface, he gave up and boarded the boat. I spent the next 30 minutes hearing only my own breathing and swimming with tropical fish and a couple of turtles. I loved every second of it. The fish became even more abundant when my youngest was tasked with throwing scraps off the boat, attracting hundreds of fish. I snapped as many underwater photos as I could, but then just wanted to live inside the sound of my hollow breath, enjoying the calm rocking of the water and semi-solitude. I'm an Aquarian on the cusp of Pisces: I love water and the life it sustains. But I also love the lush green of Hawaii.

"Can we all take snorkeling lessons before we come back?" I asked. "I think we should all learn how to snorkel so I don't have to go out alone like I did last year."

"Sure," my husband said.

As we headed through the Koko Head district, I thought *I could live here, with the Koko Head crater in my backyard.* Ocean across the street. Little shopping districts with everything you could possibly need. Homes where you can see the pride of ownership through the neat yards and flowering trees. It's utopian suburbia. The drive along the coastline is peppered with beaches, rocky outcrops, volcanic rock and breathtaking views at every turn. There are pull-outs all along the highway, almost all of them filled with cars parked as people step out to take in the views, investigate the landscape and get closer to the roaring waves. As we approached the Makapu'u Point parking lot, cars were parked on the shoulders on both sides of the highway.

"Looks like a lot of people had the same idea," Jeff said.

"Let's try the parking lot and see if we get lucky," I said.

As we rounded the final bend, the parking lot and the path came into view. Instantly, my mood shifted from peaceful anticipation to fear and anxiety. Before us was the initial climb of the trail, straight uphill, a long path that, if it were flat, could be an airplane landing strip. From the perspective of the lower parking lot, it looked impossible. Overwhelming.

A pit formed in my stomach and my negative self-talk started immediately. *I'm never going to be able to do this. I'm going to struggle every step of the way.* The path disappeared at the top as it turned toward the mountain. I held on to the hope that the trail turned flat around the corner. Jeff sensed my breathing had changed. Without me having to say a word, he knew that I was in deep consideration. I was mentally trying to navigate how to pull almost 300 pounds up that hill. I wanted to cry, but I couldn't let my kids see that I would throw in the towel before I even got out of the car.

"You can wait down here if you want," Jeff said.

"Not a chance," I said. "We came out here to do this, and we're going to do this. I'll take my time, lots of breaks. Please don't wait for me. I need to get there at my own pace."

We were fortunate to find a parking space in the lot, a small mercy, because I knew that at the end of this hike, I would be grateful for not having to climb any further to a car parked up the hill on the road's shoulder. Sunscreen was applied, hats were donned, water was in hand. Off we went.

The climb was excruciating for me, physically and emotionally. People of different sizes and ages passed me. There was a speck or two of shade cast by a cluster of skinny trees on the hillside. Taking a break in the climb, I pulled my camera out and I took photos of the vista out to the ocean. My kids, who were well ahead of me, came back down to check that I was OK. I made a show of taking photos of Koko Crater and the vista over the ocean, fooling myself into thinking that everyone else on the trail didn't notice the fat girl having to rest every 10 feet. I was getting tired, my legs were heavy, my breathing was laboured and I was only about 30 feet up the hill. I pushed on, knowing that I could rest when I got to the top, that when I turned the corner, the path would level out. Like the Little Engine That Could, I told myself *I think I can do this*. The heat from the sun was bearable because we were on the windward side of the island and the cooling breeze from the ocean was constant. I stopped to take little sips of water, knowing I had to make it last for the next two miles.

When I finally reached the top of the hill, I was physically devastated. I stood still, and felt my body tilt backward. I was weak with fatigue, a little sweaty and feeling the unforgiving pull of gravity. But it's what I saw ahead of me that made me want to cut and run. More hill. Switchbacks, which were all uphill. All uphill. ***All uphill***.

I could see the path as it wound its way up the side of the mountain. I could see people, fit people, leaning into the climb, working hard. I could feel the tears burning in my eyes. How the fuck was I going to do this?

Jeff was 100 yards ahead, waiting. He came down to me and asked if I wanted to stop and return to the car.

"Not a chance," I said. "If I give up now, I'll never push through anything hard. We've come to see the lighthouse, and I'm going to see the lighthouse. I'll take my time, take plenty of breaks. You just keep going. I'll get there when I get there. I'm never going to lose this weight if I just keep giving up." I repeated that to my kids, telling them that nothing can change if we don't try.

I pushed onwards. It was a punishing exercise. I took a pause at every opportunity. The mental ping-pong in my head kept me going. *I'm too fat — I'll never make it — I can do this — I have to start somewhere — how much farther — there are seniors passing me, for fuck's sake — how did I let this happen to me — the view will be worth it — I don't give up easily — how am I going to lose 100 pounds — I will do Diamond Head next year with 100 pounds less.* The words replayed in my head with every step, like they were on a loop. I tried to focus only on my breathing, but it was heavy and erratic. The wind was strong, so not only did it drown me out, it also made the climb that much harder.

And finally, I could see the summit. I could see the end of the trail. In some sick joke, the people who paved this crazy uphill trail thought to deal the final insult: 12 stairs up to the lookout point. I found that last reserve of strength and when I got to the platform, it was worth every bit of effort. The views brought tears to my eyes. Blues of every hue in the ocean. Rabbit Island and the smaller Kaohikaipu posing in Pacific perfection for photo opportunities. The wind was whipping around us, keeping us cool and wrapping us in ocean air. It was one of those moments in my life where I ran through a wheel of emotions: amazement, gratitude, relief, victory and resolve. I did this. I fucking reached the top.

33 WHACK-A-MOLE

While amusement parks are now a different experience for me, I still love going to the carnival. The sounds, the lights, the food — it is all part of the experience. In Toronto, the end of summer is marked with the start of the Canadian National Exhibition, two weeks of outdoor entertainment. I went a couple of times with my father, and he let me play games and win crappy stuffed animals. We ate our way through the samples in the food building. I rode The Zipper and walked around the rest of the day feeling like I was going to puke. Throughout my teens I went to Canada's Wonderland and looked forward to the end of the day, when I was done riding and could safely indulge in the deep-fried doughy funnel cakes sprinkled with icing sugar without fear of throwing up. Just after we were married, my husband and I discovered The Bloomin' Onion at the Erie County Fair. It was deep-fried nirvana.

And now, I am passing on the carnival love to our boys. Our kids had their first corn dog at the Calgary Stampede. They look forward to mini doughnuts and taking on the rides until they cannot walk straight. We let them play a few games, and watch them try their best to win a tiny stuffed toy. My favourite game is Whack-a-Mole, but I've never once played the game. I was either too intimidated by the skilled players or too broke to play. I watched the players from the sidelines. I can anticipate where the moles are going to emerge. I can feel the smack of the cloth-covered, oversized stuffed mallet travelling up my arms as if I swung it myself. I imagine it must be satisfying to feel the reverberations of the hammer as it hits the little mole head.

Those sturdy little moles are like my life. I've been pounded on, relentlessly, repeatedly, and somehow, the only major injury I've sustained is my reliance on food. I take hit after hit, and still I pop my head out of the hole to have a look around. I know how to avoid pain by ducking back into the safety of the pit. I have dents and scratches and permanent damage, but still I persevere.

The game play and combinations are endless. We've all felt like that little mole, but it's how we recover from each hit of the hammer that helps us move forward. I don't care about the size of my clothes, I just want to climb the stairs without huffing and puffing and feeling pain. I want to bend down to pick up my keys and not feel like my fat will choke me. I want to ride my bike and not be afraid that I will bend the frame or flatten the tires.

My journey is ongoing. Anyone who has ever been obese, or is still struggling, knows how this feels. It's exhausting. It's consuming — pun not intended. We know things must change, but we are overwhelmed simply by the thought of taking that first step.

I want you to know you will get over this hurdle too. One day, you will wake up and be ready for change. When you are feeling your lowest, remember this: We are all moles. No matter your size, you have been continually whacked on the head, and you keep trying to see what's out there. Keep popping out, my friends.

Dana Goldstein

ACKNOWLEDGMENTS

No one ever really reads the acknowledgements unless they know their names will be there or they have reason to hope their names will be there. I have so many people who have watched this book come to be and I thank all of you for being a part of this journey.

To my husband Jeff, who gave me as much time as I needed to get this thing done. He cooked, cleaned and took care of the kids while I toiled. Sorry ladies, he will not be returning to market any time soon.

To my clever son, Mason, who is so much like me — in personality and intelligence — that sometimes we can't communicate without fighting. You made me a mother, kid, and let me screw up without judgment. I will always share my chips with you. Maybe.

To my funny son, Westin. Lucky kid, you inherited my quick wit. That will take you far and make everyone you meet love you. Except for the ones who will hate you because you are smarter and funnier than they are.

Thank you Zoey Duncan, the editor who made this book so much better than the draft I handed off to her. She may not remember this, but Zoey and I began our working relationship when she and I discussed the possibility of a documentary about women's roller derby, a sport with which she is still actively involved. While the documentary did not happen (yet), I am grateful to the universe for placing her in my path again when I was searching for an editor.

Kirsten Wreggitt, my business and book soul sister. Kirsten and I have had similar paths in life, work and authorship. She was further ahead on the book track when I started writing this book, and she has been a guide, a beacon and a trusted, cherished friend. Do me a solid and buy her book, *Before I Let You Go: Stories For My Grown Son,* available on Amazon.

Jaime Wedholm, the wunderkind who designed the cover. I've watched Jaime's growth as a graphic designer and have absolute confidence in her work. If you don't like the cover, it's not her, it's you.

To all my online friends and those I embrace in real life. To all the people who were mean to me, or gave me a hug when I needed it most. To all of you wonderful people who came into my life, who left a mark in my memory, and whose voices I sometimes heard as I typed my words. I love you all, no matter the role you played.

ABOUT THE AUTHOR

Dana Goldstein grew up near the northern border of the city of Toronto. She has written feature stories for newspapers and magazines in Canada and the United States.

The Girl in the Gold Bikini is her first published book. She is currently working on a series for boys ages 8-12.

Dana now lives in Calgary, Alberta, Canada with her husband, two sons and their neurotic and eerily human-like dog.

93853631R00121

Made in the USA
Columbia, SC
24 April 2018